About Island Press

Island Press is the only nonprofit organization in the United States whose principal purpose is the publication of books on environmental issues and natural resource management. We provide solutions-oriented information to professionals, public officials, business and community leaders, and concerned citizens who are shaping responses to environmental problems.

In 2005, Island Press celebrates its twenty-first anniversary as the leading provider of timely and practical books that take a multidisciplinary approach to critical environmental concerns. Our growing list of titles reflects our commitment to bringing the best of an expanding body of literature to the environmental community throughout North America and the world.

Support for Island Press is provided by the Agua Fund, The Geraldine R. Dodge Foundation, Doris Duke Charitable Foundation, Ford Foundation, The George Gund Foundation, The William and Flora Hewlett Foundation, Kendeda Sustainability Fund of the Tides Foundation, The Henry Luce Foundation, The John D. and Catherine T. MacArthur Foundation, The Andrew W. Mellon Foundation, The Curtis and Edith Munson Foundation, The New-Land Foundation, The New York Community Trust, Oak Foundation, The Overbrook Foundation, The David and Lucile Packard Foundation, The Winslow Foundation, and other generous donors.

The opinions expressed in this book are those of the author(s) and do not necessarily reflect the views of these foundations.

Investing in Nature

For ERic
Thanks for your support
of TNC!
Bill G___

Investing in Nature

Case Studies of Land Conservation in Collaboration with Business

William J. Ginn

W___ G___ '08

⬤ **ISLAND**PRESS

Washington • Covelo • London

Copyright © 2005 William J. Ginn

All rights reserved under International and Pan-American Copyright Conventions. No part of this book may be reproduced in any form or by any means without permission in writing from the publisher: Island Press, 1718 Connecticut Ave., NW, Suite 300, Washington, DC 20009.

ISLAND PRESS is a trademark of The Center for Resource Economics.

Library of Congress Cataloging-in-Publication data.

Ginn, William J.
    Investing in nature : case studies of land conservation in collaboration with business / William J. Ginn.
        p.   cm.
    Includes bibliographical references and index.
    ISBN 1-59726-013-4 (pbk. : alk. paper) — ISBN 1-59726-012-6 (cloth : alk. paper)
        1. Land use, Rural—United States—States—Planning—Case studies.
2. Nature conservation—United States—States—Case studies.   3. Open spaces—United States—States—Finance—Case studies.   4. Conservation of natural resources—United States—States—Finance—Case studies.   5. Business enterprises—Environmental aspects—United States—States—Case studies.
6. Public-private sector cooperation—United States—States—Case studies.
I. Title.
    HD205.G56 2005
    333.76'16—dc22   2005013359

British Cataloguing-in-Publication data available.

Printed on recycled, acid-free paper   ∞

Design by Paul Hotvedt
Manufactured in the United States of America
10 9 8 7 6 5 4 3 2

Contents

List of Figures, Tables, and Boxes ix
Acknowledgments xiii

Introduction
The Scale of Nature 1

Part 1
Conservation Investment Banking 15

Chapter 1
Partnering with Big Timber 17

Chapter 2
Debt for Nature: The Story of the Katahdin Forest 42

Chapter 3
Bankruptcy and Biodiversity 53

Chapter 4
Investing with an Attitude 63

Part 2
Creating New Environmental Markets 73

Chapter 5
Carbon and Forests 75

Chapter 6
The Bank of Nature 92

Part 3
Incentives   105

Chapter 7
Greening Business   107

Chapter 8
Tax Credits for Conservation   119

Chapter 9
Incentives for Working Landscapes   136

Part 4
The Path Forward   155

Chapter 10
If You Build It, Will They Come?   157

Chapter 11
Conservation at the Scale of Nature   168

Chapter 12
Crossing the Divide   181

Notes   185
Bibliography   191
Index   201

List of Figures, Tables, and Boxes

Figures

Figure I.1 Furbish's lousewort *Pedicularis furbishiae*   2

Figure I.2 St. John River, Maine   3

Figure I.3 Federal Land Conservation Spending   6

Figure 1.1 IP's Connecticut Headwaters Property, New Hampshire   18

Figure 1.2 Connecticut Headwaters: Unbundling the land rights   21

Figure 1.3 Major Buyers and Sellers of Timberland, 2004   24

Figure 1.4 Map of Tug Hill, New York   29

Figure 1.5 Map of Spring River   32

Figure 2.1 The Katahdin Forest, Maine   44

Figure 3.1 Chile's Valdivian Coast   54

Figure 3.2 Trillium's Rio Condor Project   59

Figure 4.1 Map of the Fishing Grounds, Gulf of Maine   65

Figure 5.1 Noel Kempff National Park   76

Figure 6.1 The Malpai Borderlands   94

Figure 6.2 How Grassbanks Work   96

Figure 6.3 Clinch River Timber Bank   102

Figure 7.1 Canada's Boreal Zone   111

Figure 7.2 Great Bear Rainforest   112

Figure 8.1 Kelda's Decision Calculus   123

Figure 8.2 Using New Market Tax Credits for Conservation   131

Figure 10.1 Virginia's Eastern Shore   159

Figure 10.2 Major Threats to the Josephstall-Madang Province, Papua New Guinea   165

Figure 11.1 The Northern Forest   169

Figure 11.2 Northern Forest Biodiversity Strategy   171

Figure 11.3 Scaling Factors for Reserves in the Northern Forest   174

Figure 11.4 Major Conservation Projects, 1990 and 2002   179

Tables

Table I.1 Field Guide to Market-Based Tools for Conservation   12

Table 1.1 Major Timberland Owners   23

Table 1.2 Major Institutional Investors in TIMOs and REITs   26

Table 1.3 Comparing Connecticut Headwaters with the St. John
Purchase   28

Table 1.4 Fish Creek Project—Tug Hill, New York   31

Table 5.1 Maine Forestry Greenhouse Gas Savings   84

Table 5.2 Sampling of State and Regional Efforts to Control Climate
Change   89

Table 8.1 Summary of State and Federal Income Tax Credits for Conservation,
April 2003   132

Table 9.1 Outlays for Mandatory Agricultural Incentive Programs   142

Boxes

Box 1.1 Key Concepts in Partnering with Private Capital   34

Box 1.2 Field Guide to the Timber Investment Organizations   36

Box 2.1 Debt for Nature   50

Box 3.1 Conservation Investment Banking   62

Box 4.1 Investing with an Attitude   71

Box 5.1 Working on Forest Carbon Issues   86

Box 5.2 Resources for Carbon Projects   88

Box 6.1 Model Grassbanking Projects   97

Box 6.2 Resources for the Bank of Nature   103

Box 7.1 Forest Certification Resources   118

Box 8.1 Ways to Utilize New Market Tax Credits for Conservation   129

Box 8.2 Tax Credits and Incentives   130

Box 9.1 Environmental Quality Incentives Program (EQIP) Projects   140

Box 9.2 Center for Conservation Incentives, Environmental Defense
Fund   143

Box 9.3 Federal Government Programs   144

Box 10.1 Lessons about Compatible Development   167

Box 11.1 Major Land Conservation Transactions—Vermont, New Hampshire,
and Western Maine   176

Box 11.2 Northern Forest Resources   180

Acknowledgments

For many years in the early spring we drove from my home in suburban Cleveland to rural eastern Pennsylvania where my grandparents lived. My grandfather operated a small truck farm and tended apple orchards in the area while delivering bread door to door. I spent my days wandering on the well-worn forest paths behind their farm, free for a change from the pavement and grids of suburbia. On warm spring mornings I sat with my grandfather by the woodpile while he showed me how to identify the rich red grain of oak, the smooth creamy maple grain and the coarse texture of the occasional pine log. I thought then, how extraordinary to know such things. Later, when nearly eighty years old, my grandfather fell out of an apple tree he was pruning and never really recovered. I can't think of a better way to go. I still smile when I split wood behind my own barn and think of him, my namesake.

On one of my last trips before my grandfather passed away—I was about ten years old—I discovered a new subdivision of pastel-colored houses pushing into the back of the woods in neatly cleared lots—suburban Philadelphia was even then encroaching on the ring of small farms around the city. I had no vocabulary to express my feelings—Earth Day was still ten years away and words like *environment* and *biodiversity* were unknown to me. Now, forty-odd years later, I still remember my profound sense of loss. This was the beginning of my environmental awakening.

I am grateful to my parents, Bill and Arlene, who were shocked when I announced that I was forsaking an elite New England college to attend a small start-up environmental school on the coast of Maine. The privilege of attending the first year of the College of the Atlantic and their support for all of my endeavors then and since has made all the difference.

Many colleagues and friends have made lasting impressions on me—
many more than I can possibly name here but I must mention a few. Dick
Anderson and Sherry Huber, my first bosses at the Maine Audubon Society took a chance in hiring me and I am grateful always for their inspi-
ration, energy, and lifelong friendship. My colleagues at Resource
Conservation Services stood by the company in some dark moments and
shared with me in our successes. In particular Sandy Wyman (who offered
to loan me back her first paycheck if it would help me keep going), Steve
Weems, Tom Rumpf, Jay Kilbourne, Jamie Ecker, Kathy Peck, Peter Cole-
man, and Jo D. Saffeir come to mind among many fine friends. Peter
Forbes of the Center for Whole Communities invited me to spend a week
with him in Vermont. His work with communities gave me new insights
on the importance of people to our environmental work.

At The Nature Conservancy, my employer of the last six years, many
have shaped and challenged my conservation preconceptions. Peter
Thomas of New Zealand took me under his wing in my first days with the
Conservancy and showed me what working with communities on conservation was all about. Kelvin Taketa, Phil Tabas, Dennis Wolkoff, Kent
Gilges, and Suzanne Case inspired me with their vision and commitment
to the Conservancy's mission. Hans Birle did the lawyering on many of
the projects I write about with creativity and absolute persistence for per-
fection. Kent Wommack taught me about dreaming big dreams. John
Cook followed his instincts in hiring me when I came back to Maine and
has mentored me though more reorganizations than I care to remember.

The support of the Conservancy and several others, in particular the
Henry P. Kendall Foundation and the Doris Duke Charitable Foundation,
has made it possible for me to be part of this great work. Many thanks
to all of their capable staff for mentoring me, but special thanks goes to
Peter Howell of Duke and now with The Open Space Institute, and Ted
Smith of Kendall for their early and unwavering support of my work.
I hope that this book will contribute to their efforts but the content and

recommendations are my own and do not imply endorsement by them or their boards.

This book would not have been possible without the help of Anne Wood whose patient early editing prevented me from committing "grammarcide," and Christopher Robinson whose splendid maps grace this book. The talented team at Island Press has made it a pleasure to complete this project.

I have been nurtured and supported by many loving friends and family along my journey. Steve and Caroline Hyde let me borrow their truck to make dump runs in the early days of my life in Maine and have been steadfast friends for nearly thirty years. My sister, Anna, and my mother-in-law, Eleanor, have been friends and unquestioning supporters forever and Ron Phillips of Coastal Enterprises continues to inspire me with his passion for equity, social justice, and sustainability. My children, Eliza and Will, have a way of cutting through the crap and getting to the point with me that I admire. I know you didn't have any choice in the matter but it's great to have you as my family.

For twenty-eight years, one person has kept the candle burning in the window on many late and lonely nights. June LaCombe, friend, confidant, moral sage, and partner, I am grateful that you liked my rhubarb pie so long ago and decided to give me a chance.

Introduction

The Scale of Nature

Perhaps it is time for the conservation movement to leave the comfort of our
past successes and direct our formidable resources toward new solutions, new
ways of thinking about our work. Nothing is harder to do because it means
making new arguments and new friends.

—Peter Forbes et al., *Coming to Land in a Troubled World*

For a flowering plant, the furbish lousewort is rather unremarkable, barely
a foot tall with small anemic, yellow flowers. As an inhabitant of the gravel
bars and ice-tossed shorelines of northern New England's rivers, however,
the lousewort loomed large in the debate over the construction of the
Dickey Lincoln Dam on Maine's rugged and remote St. John River back
in the early 1970s. On one hand, proponents of the dam pointed to its in-
consequential stature as an example of all that was wrong with the Endangered Species Act. On the other, opponents celebrated its existence as
part of the diverse fabric of a great river system. Ultimately the dam project failed, in part because of the controversy over the impact on this small
plant. Even now, thirty years later, the precedents set by the lousewort are
at the heart of our policy toward endangered species.

Protecting the lousewort from the floodwaters of the Dickey Lincoln
Dam was only the beginning of the conservation story of the St. John
River. Two decades later, The Nature Conservancy (TNC) surprised

Figure I.1
Furbish's lousewort *Pedicularis furbishiae*.

industry and government officials by purchasing nearly two hundred thousand acres of the headwaters of the St. John from International Paper for the then astonishing sum of $36 million. No one had ever attempted to raise such a large amount from private sources for conservation, but as Kent Wommack, the Executive Director of TNC's Maine Field Office, tells the story, "When we got the news that TNC had the opportunity to buy the property, we looked around the table and thought to ourselves, how could we possibly do this? But as we thought more about it we realized that the real question was, how could we possibly *not* do it."

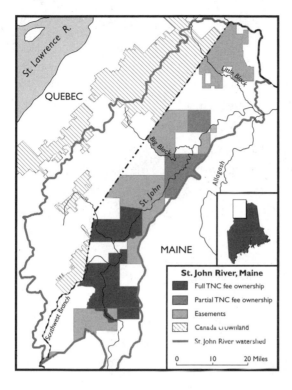

Figure I.2
St. John River, Maine.

A series of subsequent land trades, easements, and purchases over the last five years have boosted protection to over 150 miles of shoreline and over six hundred thousand acres. Because of its breathtaking size, the St. John River project is legendary in conservation circles, and it has become the standard against which many other landscape scale conservation projects are measured.

Despite these Herculean efforts and over $50 million of conservation investment, assuring the long-term ecological viability of the furbish lousewort remains elusive at best. The St. John is an unusual river as North American rivers go, in that it flows almost due north toward the Canadian border. This northward track means that spring comes earlier to the southern headwaters of the river. As melt water builds northward, it often encounters frozen ice that results in massive ice jams and flooding that scour river banks and gravel bars clean of large vegetation. It's this ecology that makes it possible for the lousewort to survive against competition from raspberries, alders, and spruce trees. In a world where by all accounts we are headed toward a warmer climate—perhaps by as much as five to eight degrees—will the reduction in ice continue to favor the conditions that support the lousewort? Recent modeling from the U.S. Forest Service suggests that New England forests will be profoundly changed in a warmer world. In the next century the line of spruce and fir trees linked so closely with the image of Maine will be pushed back north of the Canadian border in most places. The St. John River may be the last bastion of this forest type in the United States.

Addressing broad scale threats to ecological systems like climate change will be extraordinarily challenging for conservation because the problem requires new skills and competencies beyond simple land acquisition. We will be required to think about people, their role in the landscape, and the systems that hold us together as communities: governments, commerce, business, and the essential cultural and human values that control so much of how we use resources.

For conservationists the message is clear. Working at nature's scale is essential. Putting fences around small patches of land will not save the lousewort. Protecting six hundred thousand acres may not save the lousewort. Even moderating overwhelming changes in our climate will not prevent the catalog of extinction from growing. Only by being successful at *all* of these scales will the lousewort, and the millions of other species of plants, insects, and animals—from the charismatic right whales to the lowly ants—be truly protected.

The great challenge to working at the scale of nature is that a competing system is operating at the same global scale. Its power is challenging the fabric of our natural systems. The nearly irresistible forces of business and commerce increasingly dominate culture, politics, and even our natural environment. Unless we are prepared to confront the direction of the global economy, our conservation efforts will fail.

Since 2000, over 3.1 million new houses have been built in the United States.[1] The decline in forestland in the last fifteen years to make way for this and other development has been alarming. North Carolina has lost over 1 million acres of forest to clearing and conversion to development and even in rural Maine nearly 200,000 acres were developed in the period.[2] And in the year 2002, the U.S. economic engine generated $11 trillion worth of goods and services alone.[3] At the base of the American and every other world economy is the use of nature's resources—land, timber, soil, water. In a world with a population headed from over 5 billion to at least 9 billion, the pressure on our natural systems will grow even greater.

Now compare those realities with the funds available for investing in conservation. In 2005 the U.S. government will spend a paltry $314 million to expand its parks and protect wildlife refuges, national forests, and shorelines.[4] Groups like TNC, Trust for Public Lands, and the Conservation Fund raise millions more from private donors, and while these efforts may double the amount available from government, but the combined sums remain woefully inadequate. Then one must factor in the plight of biodiversity hotspots like Papua New Guinea and Indonesia. With much of their populations living at a bare subsistence level, funding for conservation is a low priority for governments dealing with faltering economies and crises in health care and education. Here the forces pushing development make the tools of conservation seem weak and wholly inadequate to the task ahead.

These are not new thoughts or statistics—and it is easy to be discouraged. But against these odds, a small group of dedicated business people turned environmental entrepreneurs and conservation-oriented investment bankers are pioneering a new set of market-based conservation tools in partnership with business. These practical visionaries have protected

Federal Agencies (millions of dollars)

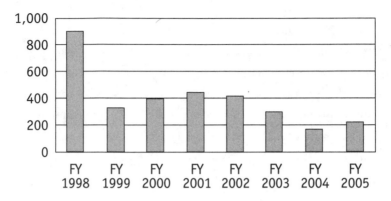

Figure I.3

Federal Land Conservation Spending. (Source: Jeffery Zinn. "Funding Trends":4–10.)

millions of acres of land; transformed the practices of entire industries; and inspired farmers, forest owners, and ranchers to change their management practices to sustain natural systems.

This book is about these new approaches. Rooted in understanding business values, economics, and motivations, these tools for conservation, powerful and practical, have shown that they can focus business on conservation at nature's scale.

I first started thinking about the ideas in this book back in 1976 when I was managing a public referendum campaign in Maine to require returnable containers for beer and soft drinks. It was a bitter battle with an array of well-funded supermarkets and beverage companies spending nearly fifteen times the small sum our rag tag army could muster. Despite the lopsided balance of funds, the legislation passed with the largest plurality of any referendum in Maine's history. In the first year of operation over 500 million bottles and cans found their way out of the landfills and off the roadsides, all because of a five-cent incentive. Five cents is such a small sum in today's economy that I still find it remarkable that two decades after implementation, over 90 percent of all containers are returned in Maine for reuse or recycling. That is powerful conservation achieved through a very modest incentive.

Increasingly, conservationists are turning toward incentives as a major tool to encourage businesses to change practices and commit to sustainable management of their resources. These tools rely not only on regulation, but also on growing customer expectations. New focus is being placed on green products harvested legally in sustainable ways, on tax credits and deductions that reward investments in conservation, and on a new set of financial incentives designed to encourage business practices and investments that support biodiversity.

But these are not the only opportunities for new approaches. Another group of investment bankers turned conservationists is aggregating capital contributed by conservation-minded individuals and organizations. These investment practitioners are buying conservation properties from bankrupt companies, restructuring corporate loans conditioned on conservation outcomes, and partnering with environmentally responsible investors to purchase vast acres of farms and forests that otherwise would be developed and in the process lost to the working landscape.

Back in 1976 we were justifiably proud of the success of Maine's bottle-deposit legislation in diverting waste from landfills. But in truth, all of the bottles and cans in Maine amount to less than 3 percent of the waste stream. A victory for sure, but was it at the scale of the problem? A few years later I had a second chance to work on waste issues, but this time as a businessman. It was this experience that opened my eyes to the power of capital, entrepreneurship, and business to effect change.

Like many of my cohorts I had arrived in Maine a decade earlier, filled with the zeal and energy behind Scott and Helen Nearing's vision of small farms and vibrant rural communities. Although my day job at that time was as executive director of the Maine Audubon Society, my wife and I clung to our agrarian vision on a small hillside farm, where we spun wool and sold spring lambs to anyone with a checkbook. In the search for more land we had the chance to farm a fifty-acre parcel not far from our home. In our first year of plowing and reseeding we had little to show from countless hours of fieldwork. Anyone with a day's worth of agricultural experience could have told us that the reason for our stunted crops was the extreme acidity of the soil, the result of years of neglect. A friendly extension agent finally took me aside and sent me out to buy lime. I was in for a rude awakening. At five tons of lime per acre and fifty acres in my field, we needed seven thousand dollars, more than half of our annual income!

A few days later, I noticed an article in the paper about a nearby mill owned by the S. D. Warren Company that had just started up a new wood-fired boiler to burn sawmill wastes. Old-time wisdom has it that recycling wood ash from the stove onto the garden sweetens the soil. Could we get wood ash, and in enough volume, to do the same on our fields?

I happened to know this mill very well. Anyone growing up in southern Maine lived with the smell of the Warren mill. For years the company had been paying to wash smoke stack soot from cars and repaint houses to keep a restless peace with the community. Ironically, one of my first jobs at Maine Audubon was cleaning up a pile of broken bags of lime and pallets on a field overlooking the Presumpcot River that had been used by the company as a helicopter pad in the summer to spread lime on the banks of the estuary to kill the smell of the mill's polluted waters. When I called Ray Pepin, the director of environmental affairs at the mill, he sounded harried and frustrated. Yes, he had ash—a lot of ash—in fact forty thousand yards a year of ash—and he didn't mind telling me that it was going to cost the company $5 million a year to truck it to Massachusetts—if they could get a permit.

Later that spring, trucks showed up filled with "bioash" to be plowed into our soil. The results of our little experiment were nothing short of miraculous. Where brown and wizened grass had barely survived in previous years, a thick carpet of green emerged. It was clear that we were onto something.

Later that fall I went over to the mill to meet with management to evaluate the project. The mill manager liked what he saw but he wasn't very excited about sending mill workers out into the community to find other farmers like me with whom to work with. I went home that night and told my wife that I had a business idea—finding farmers to take useful waste products and use them for fertilizer. In the first year after I quit my job at Audubon, my new company, Resource Conservation Services Inc., grossed just $24,000 in revenue but in ten years we were marketing and selling over $8.5 million worth of waste products, not just in Maine but throughout most of New England and New York.

In that first year, from one mill we recycled nearly the same amount of waste as my returnable container law was achieving from the combined efforts of over 1 million people. In 1992, when I sold the company to a large solid-waste concern, we were recycling over a million yards of waste a year at a handsome profit. That was more than twenty-five times what I had achieved in the previous decade of policy work, referendums, and legislation. I was hooked on the role of entrepreneurs, private capital, and market forces in being able to achieve something vastly more significant than I had ever dreamed of as a fledgling environmentalist.

But the opportunities for conservation have not stopped at new incentives or investment approaches. Another group of entrepreneurs has been tackling the task of creating wholly new marketplaces for environmental goods and services. Their vision has resulted in forest conservation projects as a source for carbon credits. They have developed natural resource–based "banks" where the currency is not money but grass, water, or timber resources. Conservationists are setting in motion powerful new approaches to engage business in the business of biodiversity.

As in any new field, this is an evolving story and not all of the recipes for conservation have been perfected or even shown to work at all. Indeed I'll be talking about failures also in the hope that we can learn from the trials of The Nature Conservancy's Virginia Eastern Shore Corporation or my own work with sustainable forestry in the South Pacific. As any entrepreneur knows, the risk of failure comes with the territory and to think otherwise is foolish. We have a lot to learn from our mistakes and we need to be honest about what works and what does not.

Now, over ten years have passed since the sale of my company and I labor again in the conservation vineyard. This time around my focus is on a new set of tools to achieve conservation at the scale of nature. My message is simple—markets and market-based conservation tools are powerful complements to old-fashioned land conservation. In an era of dwindling public resources and even scarcer charitable dollars, these new tools, honed from years in business and adapted by a growing group of entrepreneurial conservationists, are showing a new pathway to achieve our biodiversity goals.

But the importance of engaging business in the environment is not only about being clever in structuring land deals—it goes far beyond—to the heart of why we are protecting natural systems. The future of our planet is at stake. Communities are organized around economic systems and we can't defeat human nature. We are a species that thrives by trading and thereby sharing goods and services—it is this collaboration for survival that distinguishes us from other species. Our future will be determined by whether we can find ways to use these skills to enhance the quality of life and the relationships between people and the natural systems of earth. The other choice is for our era to be recorded as the last feeding frenzy over the dwindling resources of the fossil fuel age. Commerce, properly incentivized and structured is perhaps our best hope for a tool powerful enough to create and sustain communities in a new harmony with the rest of the biodiversity of this planet.

In the chapters that follow I have organized my exploration of new tools for partnering with business into four sections. In each chapter in these sections I will present a cluster of new practical ideas for land conservation based on real examples that I or my colleagues have been working on. My purpose is to provide not only insights into how business thinks about conservation decisions but also to go beyond philosophy with practical tips on how to conceive and implement these strategies.

In Part 1, "Conservation Investment Banking," I will explore interesting partnerships with private capital, conservation-oriented lending, and the adroit use of investment banking tools that have resulted in some extraordinary conservation results. Investment banking is about finding and deploying capital to grow businesses. Arranging loans, merging and acquiring businesses, investing in or creating new companies and partnerships to take advantage of marketplace opportunities—all are tools of the investment banking trade. *Conservation* investment banking is a new specialty that, like its kindred soul socially responsible investing, is focused on using capital to obtain conservation results while also meeting business needs.

In Part 2, "Creating New Environmental Markets," we will look at the new markets for nature's goods and services that have been used to conserve millions of acres of land. The topics range from using carbon credits to protect forests even in this uncertain "post" Kyoto period, and the creation of natural resource–based "banks"—grassbanks, forest banks, and water banks—all deployed around land conservation objectives.

The concept of *incentives* is the focus of Part 3. Here we will look at how working with customer demands for green products, harvested sustainably, has moved some of the world's largest companies into new conservation-oriented land management practices. We will also explore new tax credits and deductions that encourage companies to do the right thing. Finally, we will look at financial incentives for conservation—grants and payments linked to conservation management—that encourage companies and landowners to manage for endangered species and implement wildlife conservation practices.

In Part 4, "The Path Forward," we will explore some things that have not worked for conservation groups—failed projects that give insight. At

Table I.1

Field Guide to Market-Based Tools for Conservation

		Page
Conservation Investment Banking		
Swapping debt for nature conservation	The Katahdin Project, ME	42
Partnering with private capital	Tug Hill, NY	17
	Connecticut Headwaters, NH	28
	Spring River, ME	32
	Tennessee Highlands, TN	31
Lending money linked to conservation	Fish Tags, ME	63
	The Katahdin Project, ME	42
Environmentally and socially	Lyme Timber Company	67
responsible investors	Conservation Forest Partners	69
Working with bankrupt/	Valdivian Coast Project, Chile	53
defaulting companies	Trillium, Tierra del Fuego,	
	Chile	58
Developing New Markets for Environmental Services		
Carbon and forests	Noel Kempff, Bolivia	75
	Midwest Forest Restoration	
	Project, IN and OH	83
Grassbanks	Malpai Borderlands, NM	93
	Heart of the Mountains, CO	95
	Matador Ranch, MT	95
Water markets/rights	Alcoa-FERC Project, TN	100
	Stillwater NWR, NV	99
Forest banks	Clinch River Valley, VA	101
Incentives		
Green consumers	Indonesia Illegal Logging	
	Project	108
	Canadian Boreal Forest	
	Initiative	110
	Great Bear Rainforest	111
	TI Paperco, Inc., ME	116

Table I.1 (continued)

		Page
Tax credits—state initiatives	Kelda-Bridgewater Hydraulics, CT	119
New Market Tax Credits	TNC-CEI Partnership	127
Federal incentives	Farm Bill programs	139
	Landowner incentive programs	138
	Safe Harbor agreements for endangered species	139
The Path Forward		
Compatible development initiatives	Virginia Eastern Shore Corporation	157
Biodiversity support network	Josephstall Forest project, Papua New Guinea	163
Landscape scale initiatives	Northern Appalachian Ecoregion, ME, VT, NH, NY, Canadian Maritimes, Quebec	168

least one of these efforts, The Nature Conservancy's controversial compatible development approach in Virginia, has faced scrutiny from the press and donors. We will also step back and see the hopeful signs of what ten years of working on these new conservation strategies is accomplishing in the northern Appalachians of Vermont, New Hampshire, and western Maine.

As E. O. Wilson observed, "The juggernaut of technology-based capitalism will not be stopped, but its direction can be changed."[5] This book is about changing the direction of conservation *and* business in ways that can save our natural capital—land, water, biodiversity—while honoring the energy, creativity, and power of both.

Part I
Conservation Investment Banking

1

Partnering with Big Timber

The record clearly shows that conservation can't succeed by charity alone. It has a fighting chance, however, with well designed appeals to self interest. The challenge now is to change the rules of the game so as to produce new incentives for environmental protection, geared to both society's long-term well-being and individual's self-interest.

—Gretchen Daily and Katherine Ellison, *The New Economy of Nature*

When rumors of a gigantic sell off of forestlands by International Paper (IP) reached the state capital in Concord, New Hampshire, it set off alarm bells in Governor Jean Shaheen's office. At nearly 4 percent of the entire state, such a land sale was bound to get attention, and New Hampshire's fragile North Country economy was already suffering. Months before, the paper mill complex in Berlin and Gorham had filed for bankruptcy and was shuttered. For the first time in a hundred years paper machines stood idle, putting one thousand mill and forest workers out of jobs and undermining the local economy. The timing of a sell-off could not have been worse.

Working quickly, the governor and the state's powerful senior U.S. senator, Judd Gregg, arranged for high-level meetings at IP's Stanford, Connecticut, offices. Still a major land and mill owner in the Northeast, IP recognized that the political fallout of not working with the state would

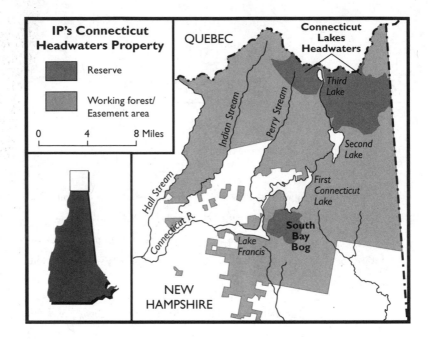

Figure 1.1

IP's Connecticut Headwaters Property, New Hampshire.

be significant so they gave their grudging agreement to a few months' stay. A consortium of conservation groups, led by the Trust for Public Land (TPL), was designated by the state to lead the negotiations.

At a property valuation of over $30 million, no conservation group had nearly enough money to buy the land alone, and certainly the state, embroiled in an intense debate over education funding, was in no position to front the money. What's more, the communities in the region were wary of conservation groups that might undermine the already suffering forest economy by reducing forest productivity or reversing the long history of public use for snowmobiling and hunting.

What could have been a protracted conflict over the future of the property, however, evolved into a remarkable partnership that met both the needs of the local community for a solution honoring the long tradition of a forest-based economy, and the interests of the conservationists in protecting the property's biodiversity values. The key partners in this effort were a private investment group managed by Lyme Timber Company; the Society for the Protection of New Hampshire Forests, a savvy and capable statewide conservation group; The Nature Conservancy (TNC) with its focus on reserves and biodiversity; and the TPL, with its long experience in developing recreation access and insuring sustainable management of working landscapes.

TPL proved a good choice for managing the exhausting negotiations. Working with the community was at the heart of the challenge in northern New Hampshire. For the past decade the TPL under the leadership of Will Rogers has been shifting its focus from "doing deals" to embracing land conservation as a way to strengthen and heal divided communities. As Rogers observed, "We need to realize that the work is not about conserving places. It is about conserving people and our fellow species in the web of life. It is about helping people find a different way to live."[1]

Community members were conflicted. On one hand, they desperately wished the whole thing would go away—they had become comfortable with the status quo and feared that all of this outside interest would cause them to lose control over their livelihoods. On the other hand, they recognized that change was inevitable and the communities had a golden opportunity to shape their future. TPL's capable north country manager David Houghton and a bright, articulate forester, Charlie Levesque, hired on as the local project manager, lived and breathed this project for nearly a year, developing a relationship of trust with all of the parties. This investment in understanding the community went a long way in keeping the political coalition together that ultimately resulted in a multimillion dollar legislative appropriation and $12 million in forest legacy funding.

When the deal closed in March 2003, Lyme had put up $12 million in private capital to purchase one hundred and forty-two thousand acres of working forest; TPL had secured a working forest easement over the property, at a cost of about $15 million; and TNC had purchased twenty-five thousand acres as a wildlife management area for over $5 million for later transfer to the State with TNC retaining a conservation easement. The needs of the stakeholders for a sustainable solution that incorporated conservation shaped the transaction, and each of the partners benefited from the wholesale price negotiated with IP. But above all, the private capital investment by Lyme made the economics of the deal work.

Engineering the financial components of the deal proved challenging for TPL, the partnership's leader. Because of IP's timeline, the forest easement could not be negotiated before the deal needed to close. At that point Houghton convinced Lyme to provide its money upfront as a loan, with an agreement that the fee purchase price would be adjusted up or down once the final easement was appraised. This proved beneficial because it took nearly two full years for the details of the easement to be negotiated and for a final transfer of the easement-encumbered land to Lyme. This saved TPL the cost of commercial borrowing, and bought time in what otherwise would have been a nearly impossible schedule to meet. For its part, Lyme had the comfort of knowing its inventory of trees was growing and that it would receive forest harvest revenues during the loan period.

The Connecticut headwaters transaction is not an isolated example of working with private capital. Opportunities for conservationists to create these partnerships are significant and growing. An unprecedented sea change in corporate ownership of working forests has resulted in millions of acres of land that have suddenly become available for purchase. In some states, the challenge has been extreme. In dozens of huge transactions in Maine, over 35 percent of the entire state has changed hands in the last five years. This crisis of opportunity has been the crucible in which many interesting new conservation agreements with private capital have been forged. The strain on the resources of conservation groups and government has made working with private capital an imperative, not an option.

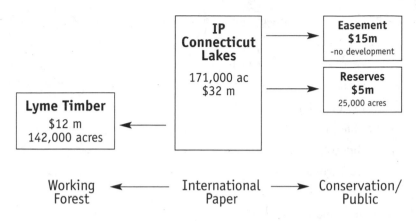

Figure 1.2
Connecticut Headwaters: Unbundling the land rights.

Since the early 1990s another reality has emerged. Over $20 billion has been invested in timber investment and management organizations (TIMOs) and real estate investment trusts (REITs). In 2003 alone, these new alliances invested $4 billion, largely from pension funds and endowments, to purchase 5.2 million acres of timberland in the United States.[2] The creation of these investment vehicles is a fascinating bit of financial history. Until the 1980s integrated paper and pulp companies owned most of the large commercial forest estates in this country. The land was viewed as essential to the supply of fiber to their nearby mills. A few major companies began to realize that they had a huge asset in their timberlands, yet they were being managed by mills interested only in reducing the costs of operating the forest holdings, not in increasing their profitability. IP and Georgia Pacific were among the first to set up their forestland holdings as separate business ventures and to expect both the mills and the forests to make a profit.

Two significant trends emerged with this seemingly subtle change in management strategy. First, forest managers could no longer look to the mills for investment cash—they had to manage the forests to make money.

Quietly, some began to sell off nonstrategic assets that were too far from markets or unproductive as tree-growing land. And, of course, selling land, especially lakeside property, to developers also generated profits without cutting significantly into the harvestable wood supply.

Secondly, mill managers, freed of buying fiber from themselves, began to find that in a global marketplace, pulp from overseas and fiber from other landowners were often cheaper. Senior managers at the major forest products companies began to question openly whether maintaining their own fiber supply made any sense. Why not buy fiber or pulp from the cheapest source and thereby increase company profitability and shareholder value?

When Hancock Life Insurance Company put together the last piece of the puzzle, the ownership transition began in earnest. The insurance company formed Hancock Timber Resources, thus putting its financial stamp of approval on a new way of owning timberlands—limited partnerships. The genius behind this idea was the recognition that the traditional paper companies pay high taxes at the corporate level and shareholders paid taxes again when they received dividends, resulting in tax inefficiencies for corporate landowners. By forming limited partnerships, "passive" tax-exempt investors such as pension funds, university endowments, and foundations could own interests in forestland directly. The profit for businesses owning forestland jumped by the amount of the tax savings—as much as 20 to 35 percent. And no more trees need be cut. Almost overnight these huge sources of capital began to look for limited partnership investments in timber.

Tax-saving benefits began to play a big part in the creation of REITs. REITs were originally set up to allow real-estate owning companies to sell shares on stock exchanges. Like limited partnerships, the ultimate recipient of the income, not the REIT, pays the tax. The objective of early REITs was to attract investment capital for commercial real estate—shopping centers and office buildings—but a group of astute businesspeople at

Table 1.1

Major Timberland Owners

1981			2004		
Company	1000's of acres	Type	Company	1000's of acres	Type
International Paper	6,900	Traditional	Plum Creek	8,060	REIT
Weyerhauser	5,900	Traditional	International Paper	7,200	Traditional
Georgia Pacific*	4,600	Traditional	Weyerhauser	6,800	Traditional
St. Regis*	3,200	Traditional	Forest Capital Asoc.	2,340	TIMO
Champion*	3,250	Traditional	Mead Westvaco	2,320	Traditional
Boise Cascade*	3,100	Traditional	Temple Inland	2,100	Traditional
Scott*	2,850	Traditional	Rayonier	1,990	REIT
Great Northern*	2,800	Traditional	GMO	1,600	TIMO
Bowater	2,000	Traditional	Forestland Group	1,540	TIMO
Crown*	2,000	Traditional	Sierra Pacific	1,532	Traditional
Union Camp*	1,700	Traditional	Potlatch	1,469	Traditional
Diamond*	1,600	Traditional	Forest Investment Asoc.	1,450	TIMO
Mead	1,550	Traditional	Hancock	1,265	TIMO
Time*	1,500	Traditional	Regions M Keegan	1,100	TIMO
Burlington Northern*	1,450	Traditional	Molpus Woodlands	1,050	TIMO

*These companies either no longer own substantial forestland or no longer exist as separate companies today.

(Source: 1981 data from Irland 2004; 2004 data from Timberland Markets, modified for recent sales by the author.)

Burlington Northern Company, a land rich railroad company, realized the REIT approach was equally applicable to owning forestland. Shareholders would have tax advantages such as limited partnerships, but also be able to simply sell or buy stock on the market without selling the forestland to get their return. Today, the successor corporation to Burlington Northern, Plum Creek, organized as a REIT, is the largest private timberland landowner in the United States, owning over 8 million acres. Thus, with powerful new tax structures and increasing recognition in the

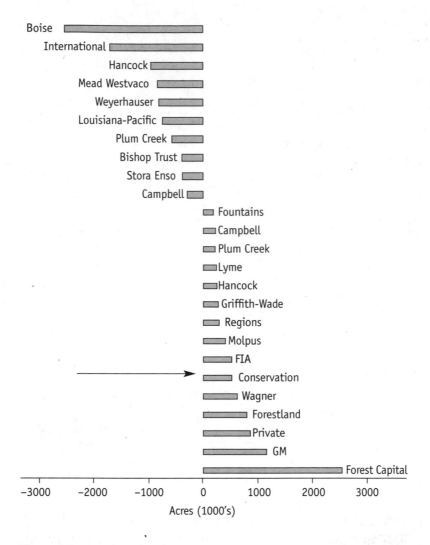

Figure 1.3

Major Buyers and Sellers of Timberland, 2004. (Source: *Timberland Markets*, 2004.)

traditional paper industry that fiber supply and land ownership were separable, the race for America's timberlands is on.

Five years ago none of the TIMOs or REITs would have appeared in a list of the fifteen largest forestland ownerships, and today the major sellers to investors continue to be traditional industrial landowners. IP owned 11 million acres in the year 2000. Now it has been eclipsed by Plum Creek as the largest forest owner.

One major difference between traditional owners and the new investors is the relatively short time the investors intended to hold their land. In 2003 new investors Plum Creek, Campbell and Hancock were the biggest buyers *and* the biggest sellers. With TIMO partnerships typically having a limited life of eight to twelve years, the exit strategy is the sale of the land. Pension funds, the largest source of capital for TIMOs, are required by law to return the highest profit to their pensioners, and that value is often achieved by splitting up the land or developing high-value shore frontage.

The industry is so new that the conservation impacts of these secondary sales have yet to be fully realized, but we have two good examples that suggest cause for alarm. In late 2002, Hancock Timber began selling off five hundred thousand acres acquired for the California pension giant CALPER. This land was bought in a handful of units over the years for CALPERs and was resold in dozens of blocks. Similarly, IP has begun to act more like a TIMO in its sales of land. In 2003, IP created a new company called Blue Sky that sold about 885,000 acres last year in an astonishing 548 separate transactions.[3] For conservationists these trends are troubling. As holdings become fragmented into smaller and smaller blocks, development, liquidation harvesting, and conversion begin to rise dramatically.

Yet this very trend makes for extraordinary conservation opportunities. Unlike the past when industrial owners spurned conservation organizations, the new owners look to conservationists as major buyers of

Table 1.2

Major Institutional Investors in TIMOs and REITS

Public institutions	California Public Employee Retirement System (CalPERS)
	State Teachers Retirement System of Ohio
	Washington State Investment Board
Private plans	Teachers Insurance and Annuity Association (TIAA-CREF)
	General Motors
	Delta Airlines
	United Parcel Service
Foundations/endowments	Harvard University
	Howard Hughes Medical Institute
	Yale University

Adapted from Nadine E. Block and V. Alaric Sample, eds., *Industrial Timberland Divestitures and Investments*, 10.

their lands. In fact conservation interests were the fourth largest buyer of forestlands in the United States in 2003.[4]

The central problem for conservationists is to avoid being a retail buyer of small parcels at a premium price while adroit TIMOs, with access to far greater capital, pick up all of the large properties on the market, giving them control of the properties' future. The solution is simple but not easy to implement. Conservationists and their allies need to be prepared to purchase the large parcels that contain properties of high conservation value within them. This allows conservation to control the deal and to set priorities for the ultimate use of the property. But purchasing large properties can be a daunting proposition. In 2003, the most expensive purchase of forestland was Campbell Group's $401 million acquisition for Mass PRIM, a pension fund, and in that year there were ten other transactions in excess of $100 million.

Assembling the conservation capital to bid on these huge projects is possible, as demonstrated by TNC's $35 million St. John purchase and the Conservation Fund's $72 million/three-hundred-thousand-acre Champion International project in New York, Vermont, and New Hampshire. Still, this is a daunting prospect for most land trusts and has not been often repeated, partly because of the new model forged in the IP Connecticut Headwaters transaction and dozens of similar deals. In these new joint ventures conservation groups and private investors have purchased properties together, sharing the risks and benefits. As in the Connecticut deal, working-forest portions of the properties, usually encumbered with easements, are transferred to the investors while key conservation assets are retained. Both parties get the benefit of wholesale transaction prices.

In TNC's purchase of the St. John's 185,000 acres in Maine, private donors contributed the entire $35 million dollars. Today TNC owns the full property and has a model demonstration forest project on ninety-five thousand acres, with the rest in reserves, where biodiversity is the main management focus. The almost identical scale purchase of the Connecticut Headwaters from IP cost $32.8 million dollars, but instead of conservation footing the entire bill, private investors provided $12 million to purchase timber rights, reducing by more than a third the conservation capital required. Here is a comparison on the two transactions.

In many cases the question of whether to buy it all or to split the cost with private capital is academic. Without private capital, most land trusts will not be able to take the financial risks in these huge projects. How these costs are shared is highly specific. In the IP Connecticut Headwaters project, TNC wanted at least twenty-five thousand acres of reserves—and was willing to raise the money. Thus the costs were more heavily weighted toward conservation than a pure easement deal. The capital from private investors will be determined by the income from forest harvesting, the timber inventory on the property, the local markets for wood products, and the conservation restrictions on harvesting and development.

Table 1.3

Comparing Connecticut Headwaters with the St. John Purchase

St. John Property, Maine	IP Connecticut Headwaters
$35 million for 185,000 acres	$33 million for 171,000 acres
Pros	*Pros*
Conservation shaped the deal and TNC retains flexibility over conservation management of 100 percent of the property	Conservation and local economy needs shaped the deal
	Conservation capital paid for only 65 percent of the deal costs
TNC has a green "endowment" of $1 million a year from timber revenues	Costs of managing timber portion of the property are borne by private investors
Cons	*Cons*
100 percent of the capital came from conservation donors	Conservation solution is locked in at beginning—reduced flexibility for the future
TNC is in the timber business on nonstrategic conservation assets	Economics of timber harvesting influenced the location of reserves, easement conditions
	No timber income to cover conservation costs

The IP headwaters transaction was preceded by a number of smaller but equally interesting transactions such as TNC's Tug Hill project, sandwiched between New York's Adirondacks and the eastern end of Lake Ontario. Tug Hill is well known for its heavy snows, averaging three hundred inches of snowfall and fifty-five inches of precipitation annually. TNC had long been eyeing a forty-five-thousand-acre parcel owned by Hancock Timber right in the geographic bull's eye of this northern hardwood landscape. Tug Hill is also one of the poorest regions in all of New York. While the Carnegies and Rockefellers lounge just over the Adirondack border, Tug Hill has attracted few tourists and even fewer philanthropic dollars

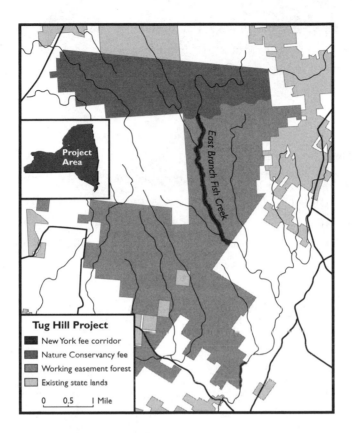

East Branch Fish Creek

Tug Hill Project
- New York fee corridor
- Nature Conservancy fee
- Working easement forest
- Existing state lands

0   0.5 | Mile

Project Area

Figure 1.4
Map of Tug Hill, New York

over the years. To make this purchase work, it was critical to use conservation dollars efficiently and to attract public funds.

Here is how the transaction was structured. TNC purchased the entire property from Hancock Timber for $9.1 million. TNC retained thirteen thousand acres as reserve land in a key area, where other New York State holdings created a block of over twenty-five thousand acres of protected areas. The State of New York took title to a 1,400-acre corridor that captures more than eight miles of the East Branch of Fish Creek, one of Tug Hill's largest rivers and the source of drinking water for several upstate cities. The balance of just over thirty thousand acres was encumbered by a working forest easement and resold to Renewable Resources LLP, a partnership managed by old-line Boston money managers Grantham and Mayo (GMO). GMO was a last minute stand in; another timber investment firm backed out at the eleventh hour because they concluded that with the heavy harvesting of the property recently completed by Hancock and its predecessor, Lyons Falls Pulp & Paper, income from the property in the short term would be small. This was a lesson in understanding the motivations of timber buyers and how they can vary from investor to investor. GMO's investors were more interested in long-term inventory growth and future income, current income was of less concern. There is no "right" answer to this investment balancing act. Some timber investment funds specialize in short-term returns from harvesting versus the longer term but potentially more rewarding capital appreciation strategies of others. As the timber investment industry matures we will begin to see companies create different investment products based on the needs of the investors much the way mutual fund companies do today. The economics of the Tug Hill transaction are shown in table 1.4.

TNC and its partner, the state, obtained critical reserve areas and protected the working landscape, for a cash investment of around 60 percent of the purchase price. A side benefit of this and similar transactions is that local communities, especially in hard-hit rural forest areas, are nearly always more supportive of a sustainable forest vision with conservation elements than they are of a pure conservation solution. That makes it easier to leverage state and federal money into the conservation part of these transactions.

On Tug Hill, continued recreational access for hunting clubs and snowmobiling also was important to gaining local acceptance and public funding. The Tug Hill Commission, a state agency, played a critical role in

Table 1.4

Fish Creek Project—Tug Hill, New York

Purchases	Cost	Percentage of Project Cost
TNC Fee: (13,000 acres)	$2.4 m	26%
NY state easement (30,300 acres)		
and corridor along Fish Creek (1,350 acres)	$3.1 m	34%
GMO-RR working forest (30,300 acres)	$3.6 m	40%
Total project	$9.1 m	

soliciting input from local residents and stakeholders to ensure that the transaction met local desires. In addition to continued recreational access, Tug Hill residents also were concerned about loss of property tax revenue from any change in ownership. As a result, the Tug Hill Commission helped enact new state legislation that required the state of New York to pay its share of property taxes on conservation easements held by the state on Tug Hill. TNC also has committed to a payment in lieu of taxes on its Tug Hill lands.

This model has been replicated in other conservation transactions across the country. One interesting permutation is a transaction completed by the Conservation Fund in Tennessee, also with GMO-Renewable Resources LLC (GMO-RR). When the Tennessee land came up for sale, the State of Tennessee wanted to own the property but didn't have enough money to buy it, so the Conservation Fund implemented a novel solution. GMO-RR purchased a perpetual timber deed granting GMO the ownership of the trees on the property and the right to manage them, but the state did not grant ownership of the underlying land. As the fee owner the state holds full title to the recreational use of the property as long as it did not interfere with carefully prescribed forest operations. Since GMO-RR did not acquire the land—only the trees, they never acquired development rights—those stay with the state.

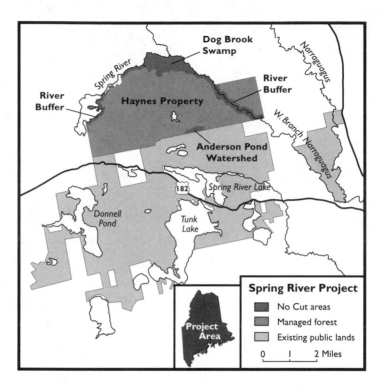

Figure 1.5
Map of Spring River

During one of the early negotiations on the purchase of IP's holdings
along the Machias River in Maine, Tom Rumpf, TNC's director of protection in Maine, and I proposed the outlines of the acquisition to the IP
team. Pat Flood, IP's real-estate manager, looked at our map and pointed
to the Spring River area and observed, "That's too bad, we just sold that
ten thousand acres to H. C. Haynes last week." Needless to say this was a
discouraging moment. Haynes has a reputation of harvesting hard and
then selling the lots to developers as rural camps. If this property went that
way, we would lose the opportunity to protect this tributary of an important salmon river in the Northeast, and to expand an important ecological reserve on state land abutting this tract.

Later Tom approached Haynes and worked out a variation on the theme of partnering with private capital. TNC agreed to purchase the Spring River property from Haynes within three years, but only after Haynes had harvested most of the valuable timber. Haynes, for his part, agreed to not harvest at all on some 1,300 acres of land along the river, and harvest more lightly than he would have otherwise been inclined on the remainder of the property. By buying the property after valuable timber was harvested we reduced the price of the property to something we could afford, and accepted a trade-off with conservation goals: harvesting would add a few decades to the recovery of the forest system. Yet it was a reasonable trade-off compared to the alternative of losing the property forever. Haynes bought the property from IP for $3 million, with TNC having a three-year option to purchase postharvesting for $2.2 million. Thus the net savings to TNC, to be balanced against the ecological values compromised, was eight hundred thousand dollars. And this is likely to be a very conservative savings as Haynes purchased the property as part of a larger package of lands for a very attractive price and the deal essentially locks today's price for the next five years.

Working with private capital requires a willingness to balance the goals of conservation with the expectations of private investors for a reasonable return on their capital. If the property is a priceless stand of old-growth trees, then traditional approaches may be the best option. On the other hand, as we move to work at the scale of nature's landscapes and ecological systems, sustainably managed working lands often can contribute to the conservation solution. Always, conservation goals must be carefully considered and structured in developing these deals.

For some conservationists, the connection with private investors will represent an unacceptable compromise. However, the specifics of the project provide the best guidance for answering this concern. Tough questions about the alternative uses for limited conservation capital have to be asked. Will partnering with private capital free existing funds for other important conservation efforts? What are the cost benefits of a pure conservation solution as against a partial one where the most intractable threats, such as development or subdivision, are eliminated? Is it also worth considering the broad benefits of introducing private investors to a whole new way of relating to the land, based on sustainable use? Maintaining and enhancing the natural resource–based economy of local communities is an essential part of creating a sustainable global economy in balance with what nature can provide. If we begin to use business as an essential connection between the livelihoods of local communities and natural systems then our efforts move us toward this broader goal. In the long run, sustainable use must become the foundation of all communities and not a conservation-inspired luxury.

Box 1.1

Key Concepts in Partnering with Private Capital

Be clear about the *conservation goals of the project*. Will working with private investors represent an acceptable trade-off for the particular lands to be protected?

The goal of partnering is to be able to *participate in the primary sale event*, instead of the aftermarket, for conservation properties. This means assembling a team of partners and working to control the deal for conservation outcomes through the bid, auction, or negotiation process

Start early to identify potential partners. If you are just coming together on the schedule of a bid or auction, you face an uphill battle to work out roles and interests of the partners.

Be careful whom you partner with. You will be known by the values of the entire team and a partner with money but questionable practices may be worse than no partner at all.

Recognize that you are providing an important service for which you
have every right to expect the full benefits of your partnership role.
By providing conservation funding up front you are *taking some of
the risks out of the transaction for private investors*—otherwise they
would be required to find conservation purchasers or development
options over a much longer time period and at a much higher risk of
failure to their investors.

Work out the economics before closing on any transaction. How will the
property be valued, what is the basis of appraising the segments of
the transaction—working forest, ranches, easements, conservation
out-sales—the more you have this work completed before the bid,
the less subject you are to being caught in the middle between a bid
price that's fixed and partners that find all kinds of reasons why your
valuation and easement ideas are wanting.

Be careful about private inurement issues—The key is to make sure that
you are getting value equal to the capital and risk that you are
undertaking. This means careful appraisal work and structuring so
that land trusts are never in a position of paying more than they are
getting in value.

Expect full transparency on partners' return expectation and their
economics. That means getting proforma and financial data as well
as giving up yours. The idea is to work together to maximize shared
benefit, not secretly plot against each other. If your partner is not
committed to transparency, then it's a sure sign that they are not
committed to a fair deal. Expect to sign confidentiality agreements
and respect their privacy on financial matters.

Engage local communities in the process of creating economic
partnerships. Communicate with the community, share the vision and
have them actively participate in the future of the property as
contractors, suppliers, or perhaps even as owners.

Box 1.2

Field Guide to the Timber Investment Organizations

Campbell Group

One SW Columbia, Suite 1700

Portland, Oregon 97258 USA

Phone: 503-275-9675

Fax: 503-275-9667

E-mail: info@campbellgroup.com

Website: www.campbellgroup.com/

U.S. only (primarily NW but also interested in SE)

Several smaller conservation transactions

Conservation Forest Capital, LLP

105 N. Second Street

Suite 233

Livingston, MT 59047

Phone: 406-222-9790

E-mail: JMTomlinMT@aol.com

New investment fund specializing in conservation oriented transaction

U.S. Focus

Forest Capital Partners, LLC

One Financial Center

Boston, MA 02111

Phone: 617-832-2922

Fax: 617-832-2921

E-mail: mdonegan@forestcap.com

Website: www.forestcap.com/

Privately held

U.S. Recently purchased all of the former Boise Cascade Timberlands in
seven states

No conservation deals at this time

Forest Investment Associates

15 Piedmont Center, Suite 1250

Atlanta, Georgia 30305

Phone: 404-261-9575

Fax: 404-261-9574

E-mail: info@forestinvest.com

Website: www.forestinvest.com/

U.S. only (Eastern U.S. but primarily in SE)

No conservation deals at this time

Forest Systems, LLP

Queset House

51 Main Street

North Easton, MA 02356

Telephone: 508-230-0400

Fax: 508-230-0401

E-mail: info@forestsystems.com

Website: www.forestsystems.com/

Privately held

U.S. only (SE, NW)

No conservation deals at this time

continued

Box 1.2   continued

The Forestland Group, LLC
One Brattle Square, 4th Floor
Cambridge, MA 02138
Phone: 617-491-0663
Fax: 617-491-2499
Website: www.forestlandgroup.com/

Privately held
U.S. only (NE, Mid-Atlantic, Southeast and South Central, Lake states)
Hardwood timberlands focus
Part of Bishop Estate transaction with TNC in Michigan and CF transaction
    in NY

GMO Renewable Resources
40 Rowes Wharf
Boston, MA 02110
Phone: 617-330-7500
Fax: 617-261-0134
E-mail: generalinquiries@gmo.com
Website: www.gmo.com/

Part of Grantham, Mayo, Van Otterloo, a privately held investment advisor
U.S., Brazil, New Zealand, and Australia
Many conservation transactions with TNC and CF

Hancock Timber Resource Group
99 High Street, 26th Floor
Boston, MA 02110-2320
Phone: 617-747-1600
Fax: 617-747-1516

E-mail: info@hnrg.com

Website: www.htrg.com/

Subsidiary of John Hancock Natural Resource Group, public corporation

Focus areas: U.S.(NW, SW), Australia

Many conservation-oriented transactions in US

Lyme Timber

16 On the Common

P.O. Box 266

Lyme, NH 03768

Phone: 603-795-2129

Fax: 603-795-4789

E-mail: info@lymetimber.com

Website: www.lymetimber.com/

Privately Held

U.S. focus

Many conservation deals, which the group considers its comparative advantage in sourcing transactions

The Molpus Woodlands Group

654 N. State Street

Jackson, MS 39202

Phone: 601-948-8733

Fax: 601-352-7463

E-mail: webmaster@molpus.com

Website: www.molpus.com/

Privately held

U.S. focus in SE, South Central

No conservation deals known at this time   **continued**

Box 1.2   continued

Plum Creek Timber Company, Inc.
999 Third Avenue, Suite 4300
Seattle, WA 98104-4096
Phone: 206-467-3600 or 1-800-858-5347
E-mail: info@plumcreek.com
Website: www.plumcreek.com/

Publicly traded REIT
U.S. focus (operates in nineteen states including most of the NE, Mid-
     Atlantic, South, Midwest, and NW)
Many conservation transactions with TNC, CF, TPL and other groups

Prudential Timber
P.O. Box 990407
Boston, MA 02199
Phone: 617-585-3500
Fax: 617-585-3501
Public Institutional Client Services
E-mail: public.investments@prudential.com
Private Institutional Client Services
E-mail: private.investments@prudential.com
Website: www.investmentmanagement.prudential.com/

Part of Prudential, a publicly held corporation
U.S. (SE and Hawaii), New Zealand
No conservation deals at this time

RMK Timberland Group
260 Peachtree, Suite 1800
Atlanta GA, 30303

Phone: 1-800-734-4667

E-mail: mkinfo@morgankeegan.com

Website: www.regions.com/

Formerly of Wachovia, a publicly held bank holding company recently sold
    to Regions Morgan

U.S. only (SE, Mid-Atlantic, and Lake states)

No conservation deals at this time

Wagner Forest Management

150 Orford Rd.

Lyme, NH 03768

Phone: 603-795-2002

Privately held

U.S. only (NE primarily)

Part of West Branch transaction in Maine with Forest Society and several
    other proposed transactions

2

Debt for Nature: The Story of the Katahdin Forest

I fear that environmental campaigns that have captured public imagination—
such as the worthy battles to save wilderness, rainforest, dolphins—have
helped foster the impression that crisis is primarily about distant places and
creatures rather than about the natural system that support our communities
and the larger human civilization.

—Dianne Dumanoski, *Rethinking Environmentalism*

Lambert Bedard, the burly CEO of Great Northern Paper Company, was the
last to arrive at the third-floor executive conference room in Millinocket.
After a few hurried introductions, he settled into his seat at the head of the
conference table and leaned back in his chair. "So," he said in his thick French-
Canadian accent, "what do a bunch of tree huggers have to say to me?" Not
exactly an auspicious beginning to our discussions with the company.

After a few sputtered minutes of background on The Nature Conservancy (TNC), I eyed Kent Wommack, the veteran director of the Maine
Field Office, with a silent plea for help. Kent picked up the presentation
with a bit of personal history. "Well, I grew up in a paper company family.
My father worked for Mead Paper Company most of his career, and the
ups and downs of the industry have been part of my life." Tim Morgan,
the CFO of Great Northern, swept up the stack of TNC cards and asked

quizzically. "Bill . . . Bill Wommack?, . . . he's your father?" Kent uttered a silent thanks to his father. "Yes. Yes, that's right. He's my dad." Tim excitedly interjected, "Why I worked for your father thirty years ago at the old Mead building in Dayton! Great guy, taught me a lot."

With this unexpected personal connection, the tension that had filled the room suddenly eased and in a few minutes we began to talk in earnest about TNC's audacious proposal to Great Northern—an offer to lend money to the struggling company in exchange for conservation of Great Northern lands.

Rumors began circulating in 2001 that Great Northern was in trouble. For over one hundred years the titan of the North dominated the Maine forest industry. Once the largest landowner in the state, with over 2.1 million acres under its domain and a brace of prosperous paper and lumber mills, the company was clearly down on its luck. The company's fortunes had been in a long slide since the mid-1980s when a series of mergers and new mill expansions had overextended the company and left it with a crushing debt load. The company was forced into the arms of a succession of larger integrated forest products companies including Georgia Pacific and Bowater. Each in turn had jettisoned assets, including much of the company's land base and its out-of-state paper mills. By the late 1990s, only the two mills in Millinocket and East Millinocket remained along with three hundred thousand acres of forest. A small group of entrepreneurs from Quebec were the only suitors for the company. Led by Lambert Bedard, they bought the company for a reported fifty thousand dollars in cash plus an outsized bank note. Now in 2001 the company's ambitious plans to modernize the mills were in trouble. Bedard began a new round of asset sales, including selling camp lots and the extensive hydroelectric facilities that power the mills, but the continuing downturn in the paper industry fueled the economic woes of the company.

Although Great Northern's landholdings were a fraction of what they once were, from a conservation perspective they were among the crown

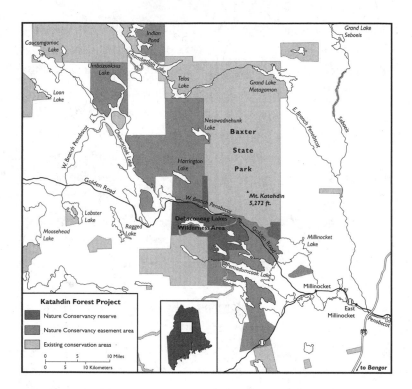

Figure 2.1

The Katahdin Forest, Maine.

jewels of the state. In the first half of the twentieth century, Governor Baxter, whose eponymous state park borders Great Northern land on the south and west, is reported to have tried many times to acquire portions of the land because of the magnificent cluster of remote lakes and ponds known as the Debsconeags—nine lakes in all, flowing into the west branch of the Penobscot River. The National Park Service had its eye on these lands as well—twenty miles of the Appalachian Trail wound its way past Rainbow and Nahmakanta Lakes on its way up the flank of Mount Katahdin, just over the park border.

A number of groups, including the Trust for Public Lands and the Wilderness Society, had approached the company about a conservation sale but each time they met with skepticism or disinterest. Concern was widespread in the conservation community, for if the company failed, the land would be auctioned off to the highest bidders to meet the needs of the creditors—and that meant development on these pristine waterways and an opportunity lost forever to add to the protected lands around Baxter State Park.

TNC had been content to let other groups work on this conservation priority, because frankly we were occupied with other priorities— purchase of the lands along the Machias River in eastern Maine and assuring the protection of the St. John River. Besides, having just finished an astonishing $52 million capital campaign, our donors were still paying off pledges on projects already underway elsewhere in the state.

Still, the fate of these lands nagged at all of us working on forest projects, and as rumors persisted about the bleak future of the company, we made our own inquires through Marcia McKeague, woodlands manager for the company. A familiar figure in Maine because of her leadership position in an otherwise male-dominated trade, Marcia was also a member of the Land for Maine's Future board, the group setting priorities from a recent $50 million bond. Marcia confirmed the company was in a delicate position. It was effectively blocked from selling any of its land. The entire forestland was collateral on a note to the Hancock Life Insurance Company, and the note had a multimillion dollar prepayment penalty designed to discourage the company from seeking better financial terms before the end of the note term. As Tom Rumpf, Maine's director of protection, Kent, and I contemplated this news in the spring of 2002, I had an inspiration. It occurred to me that if the Hancock note was the obstacle to the Great Northern sale of land for conservation, why not see if Hancock would be interested in selling the note to TNC. This exchange could open the door for Great Northern to trade debt for nature. If the company was as shaky as we thought, my reasoning was that Hancock was probably nervous as well. The amount of debt was sobering—over $46 million—but on the other hand the collateral was a conservationist dream: three hundred thousand acres of well-managed forests and undeveloped lakes and mountains in the shadow of Baxter State Park. A bank might not take the risk, given the company's situation, but the collateral had special value to TNC.

In a few hours of brainstorming we had etched out a possible approach to Great Northern, one that might be good for the company and great for conservation. The rough outlines of the plan were:

Buy the note from Hancock at a discount if at all possible, given the potential of default, but certainly without any prepayment requirements.
Trade a portion of the debt for land around the southern flank of the park, where the state's Nahmakanta public reserve lands connect with Baxter along the Appalachian Trail corridor.

However, a key problem remained. We knew that we could not afford to forgive the entire $46 million it might cost to buy out Hancock, even if Great Northern was willing to trade that many acres for debt relief. Our major supporters were still paying off their pledges on the St. John. Even for a project of this importance our best guess was that we could raise only $14 to $16 million—that left a balance of over $30 million. If we had any hope of buying out Hancock, it was clear we would have to purchase the entire note. To solve this problem we came up with a second strategy. We would offer to reloan the company the balance of the funds but at a much lower interest rate than the Hancock note—but only if the company would grant TNC a conservation easement on two hundred thousand acres of remaining lands—thus insuring that the property would be forever managed sustainably and never be given over to development. So now we had a concept but it had a lot of potential problems. Would Hancock sell the note at a rate we could afford? Would Great Northern be willing to trade land for debt relief and grant the easement?

It was this concept that brought us that spring day to the executive conference room in Millinocket to meet with Great Northern's executives. In a space of a few hours we learned how dire the company's prospects were. The company was actually already in default on its Hancock note and a group of Hancock accountants were in the next room poring over the books in preparation for foreclosure proceedings. The company urgently needed an additional $4 million to meet other cash needs. Bedard made it clear that we would need to move fast for the company to consider our offer. It was June already and the deal needed to be completed by August to save the company.

Within a few days we had assembled a business term sheet that etched out a plan. TNC would buy out the Hancock note for around $46 million and add $4 million of its own cash. Great Northern would sell forty-one thousand acres of the land in exchange for $14 million in debt relief from TNC. TNC would reloan the company $36 million dollars at 4 percent interest in exchange for a conservation easement on an additional two hundred thousand acres of the company's land.

But how to get to Hancock? We had just the man in mind. Hank Paulson, a new member of the TNC board of Governors, was chairman of Goldman Sachs and arguably the most influential businessman in America. Did he know Hancock? Would he call David F. D'Alessandro, the president, and introduce us? Within a few hours of Hank's call to D'Alessandro, I found myself talking on the phone to Ken Hines, head of Hancock's Paper and Forest Industry Finance group. Ken's laconic North Carolina accent masked a razor sharp mind for business. He drawled to me, "Bill, there's no sense getting all the top brass worked up about this, I bet you and I can just figure this out together." And true to his word, in a matter of weeks we had a deal with Hancock whereby TNC would purchase the note from Hancock for its face value of $46 million with prepayment penalties waived, but TNC needed to get the note off Hancock's books by September 30. Hancock had just gone public the year before and desperately did not want more defaulted notes on its books at the quarterly reporting period. Moody, the big business rating agency, had just downgraded Hancock's bond rating from AA1 to AA2 and the company could not afford more bad news.

The following two months were intense. We had to purchase the Hancock note, put new financing in place, acquire a huge conservation easement, take ownership of the Debsconeags, and last, but not least, get approval for all of this from TNC's state and worldwide boards to borrow an unprecedented $50 million from TNC's Land Protection Fund. On August 23, 2003, we closed the transaction and loan, and shortly thereafter we held press conferences to announce the beginning of the unlikely partnership between TNC and Great Northern.

Behind every complicated business transaction, a human story always emerges. On the day we closed, Eldon Doody, president of Great Northern, recalled his first job with the company. As a teenager he had worked as a camp boy, whose job it was to find the best fishing spots for the customers and suppliers who were guests at Great Northern's sporting camp on Rainbow Lake, now part of TNC's land. During the two summers he worked there he got to know every pond and fishing hole around. In a corporate meeting room these thirty-five years later he turned to me and said, "I'm really happy to know that this land will be just the way I remember it when I was seventeen."

The afterglow of the Great Northern deal continued into the fall but storm clouds were brewing over Millinocket. When asked at the press conference whether the TNC deal would be enough to save the company, Doody had responded that while the deal bought time for the company, what they really needed was improving markets for their products. Unfortunately for the company, the low paper prices of the last few years continued and in December Doody abruptly resigned from the company and within a few weeks the company announced that it was filing for Chapter 11 Bankruptcy protection. It became clear in the ensuing weeks that the only hope for the company was to sell itself to a stronger partner through the bankruptcy process.

These were nervous times for TNC as the reality of being the second largest creditor after the giant Boeing Leasing Company hit home. Fortunately, unlike most of the other creditors, TNC had rock solid collateral position with a first mortgage on all of the land of Great Northern and the timber owning subsidiary of Great Northern had not filed for protection in large part due to the favorable credit from TNC. Still the bankruptcy process can be unpredictable and TNC knew that other creditors were looking hungrily at the timberlands. Rather than push the timber subsidiary into bankruptcy by accelerating TNC's note as it was allowed to do in the case of the insolvency of the timber company's owner, TNC decided that the best course of action was to be patient. We felt sure that with Millinocket's new paper machine and a modern mill in East Millinocket that some suitable buyer would come along. From a conservation perspective we were comfortable with our easement on Great Northern's working forest and our acquisition of the key Debsconeag lands gave us the control over the crown conservation jewels. We also knew that many local citizens had viewed our loan with skepticism under the assumption that TNC's real plan was to put them all out of jobs and convert the area into a national park. With millions of acres left to protect in northern Maine, TNC knew that it would have to honor its commitment to allow sustainably managed working forests be part off the long-term conservation solution in the region. One false step and our creditability with other landowners and the public would be at risk. With patience TNC watched the bankruptcy process for six months until finally a new owner emerged, a Canadian-based company, Brascan Financial, who among other assets was a major owner in NexFor and Fraser Paper. With a good reputation Brascan seemed an ideal combination of deep pockets and experience in the industry. Over the next few months the mill at East Millinocket was restarted and modernization of critical parts of the Millinocket mill began. Today both mills are operating and while life will never be the same as it was when Great Northern ruled the North Country, the industry is recovering.

Out of the sale and restructuring of the mill, TNC emerged with its $36 million dollar loan to the new company back out of default. However, Brascan was not a struggling company but a financial giant with strong credit on its own and it became clear to TNC that it was time to find a way out of its loan, which was continuing to tie up capital that was needed in other conservation transactions. The innovative way TNC both honored its loan commitment and got repaid with a few months is explained in Chapter 8, when a new federal program, New Markets Tax Credits, is explained.

Box 2.1

Debt for Nature

Buying loans is an everyday practice on Wall Street. As the fortunes of companies rise and fall, banks and insurance companies regularly sell and buy defaulted notes. Groups like Goldman Sachs have entire business units dedicated to looking for gold in junk bonds. Conservation groups can play this game as well—and we have some strategic assets that commercial groups don't offer. Instead of Hancock having to announce they were putting a thousand people out of jobs by foreclosing on the company, they got to be part of a positive story of conservation and survival. That's worth something to lenders. Secondly, conservationists may have a different view of the value of collateral associated with notes. The last thing a lender wants is to have to foreclose and get property instead of cash back. In our case, we would have been happy to get land because land is our business.

Discounted Loans

One of the most interesting parts of the Great Northern transaction was offering a reduced-interest-rate loan in exchange for conservation value. At the time of this transaction, Great Northern was paying 8.73 percent interest to Hancock, plus amortizing a portion of the principal owed. Under the TNC note, no principal was owed for eight years and interest was set at 4 percent. Conservation groups are not in the business of loaning money to companies without mission-related compensation of at least equal value. To loan money to a for-profit company without achieving comparable value would be an act of private inurement and cause the charity to lose its charitable status. A critical aspect of these types of transactions will therefore be the fair evaluation of the value of the loan. In our case we calculated as follows:

Annual Payment on Hancock Note (interest and principal)	$4 million
Annual Payment on TNC Note	$1.3 million
Annual Savings	$2.7 million
Sum of savings over eight-year period	$18 million

However, because the easement was granted at the time the loan was made and the savings to Great Northern would accrue over the eight-year period it is necessary to convert the stream of savings over eight years to a value that represents the value to GNP at the same time as the easement was put in place. Economists call this calculating the "net present value" or NPV. Another way to think of this is to ask "what would you pay today for the rights to a set of payments in the future?" Your answer to this question depends a great deal on what rate of interest you expect to earn on your money. When someone wins the lottery, most often you see them take the lump sum payout which is a great deal less than the advertised sum of the thirty years of annual payments most lotteries offer. This is because they think they can earn more money on the lump sum principal over time than offered by the lottery. In our case we calculated the NPV of the sum of the savings over eight years with an interest rate of 8.73 percent—the same

continued

Box 2.1 continued

rate Great Northern was paying for its original loan from Hancock so that we could compare the value of the easement with the value of the loan.

NPV of savings @ 8.73 % $8.9 million

From this analysis we determined that the easement granted by Great Northern must be worth at least $8.9 million for us to have obtained fair value for our low-interest note. In fact when the easement was finally appraised, its value was assessed at $13 million and thus we gained extra value from the loan, offsetting concerns that risks associated with the refinancing would have demanded an even greater return.

It is critical that a careful evaluation of this issue from a financial point of view be conducted, preferably by a third party, such as a financial accountant, to insure that the value received at least equals the value surrendered.

3

Bankruptcy and Biodiversity

If you want to treat the planet as if its a business in liquidation, you can generate cash flow and the illusion of prosperity, but our children are going to pay for our joy ride. It's just deficit spending, a way of making a few people rich by making everyone poor.

—Robert F. Kennedy Jr. (Speech to the Commonwealth Club of California, February 28, 2002)

In the spring of 2003, I got an email from Margo Burnham, The Nature Conservancy's (TNC) country director in Chile, asking me if I knew anything about a Woodlands Development Corporation registered in Delaware. This company owned the debt of a failing forest company in Chile. The debt gave Woodland, along with other smaller creditors, a first mortgage on 147,500 acres of critical temperate forest on the central coast of Chile near Valdivia, one of the largest private holdings in the area. The owner, Bosques S.A., had been intent on converting these native forests to fast-growing eucalyptus trees. However, they had become mired in political and legal difficulties regarding harvesting and conversion permits, and were now in court over the validity of their permits from the Chilean National Forest Agency.

As the story unfolded in the local papers it became clear that Bosques S.A. had failed to meet its payments as environmental delays dragged on,

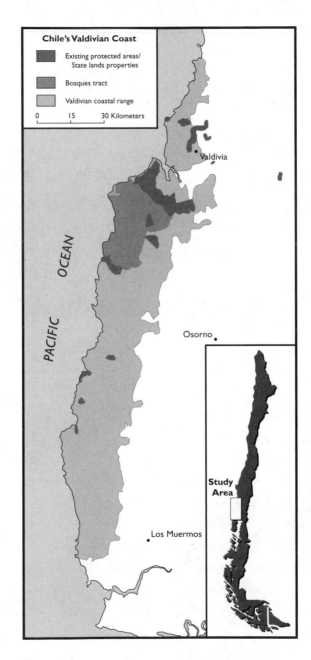

Figure 3.1

Chile's Valdivian Coast

and a consortium of lenders led by the large U.S.-based financial services company, FleetBoston, had forced the company into bankruptcy. With less than 10 percent of the property converted to plantations, this was a precious parcel of land in the thin swath of green hugging Chile's Pacific coast. For several years the property had topped the protection list of TNC and its partner, the World Wildlife Fund, as well as other environmental groups.

Saving this landscape became an immediate priority. Greg Fishbein of TNC's business consulting group and Carlos Fernandez, a sharp TNC attorney assigned to our Chilean program, were dispatched to find out what FleetBoston's plans were for the property. Yes, FleetBoston was behind Woodland Development and the private sector showed plenty of interest in buying the land. FleetBoston was not interested in a "bargain" sale of this valuable asset to TNC. But then again, if TNC wanted to discuss options with Jared Ward, one of FleetBoston's senior workout people, it would be good to get to know each other. So began an on-and-off conversation that ended in Chile's bankruptcy court.

Initially FleetBoston was cool to our interest because our offer was low and the bank was already in negotiation with another serious party in Chile that seemed more eager to take on the risks of Chile's bankruptcy process. Ed Cruchfield, former CEO of Wachovia Bank and a TNC board member, was asked to contact his friend, FleetBoston's CEO Chad Gifford, to make him aware of TNC's earnest intent. At the same time, the Rainforest Action Network (RAN) launched its own campaign against Fleet-Boston, featuring the bank on its web site and sending picketers to Boston. By making their point in a public way, the activist group hoped that Fleet-Boston would be careful in how it disposed of this property. As the summer progressed without action, Greg made a final call to Jared Ward to discuss a TNC plan. Ward, feeling pressure from the RAN campaign and his CEO, seemed interested in exploring a potential deal with TNC, but explained that FleetBoston was days away from signing a definitive agreement to sell the property to a Chilean forest investment group. Ward suggested he put TNC in contact with the Chilean group to see if they could work out a deal that works for conservation. Fishbein responded, "Why not just sell the debt to us straight out." Ward was surprised by this suggestion because until now TNC management had been reluctant to buy the debt for fear of having to engage in an uncertain bankruptcy process to get the property—a process TNC's Chilean counsel described as "rafting." Ward asked, "Can you do that? I would need a letter of intent in two business days in order to hold off the other group." Fishbein replied, "I think so, and can sure as hell try." In twenty-four hours of hasty consultations with TNC executives and board members, we came back to FleetBoston with another offer. Based on that offer, FleetBoston agreed to negotiate a deal with TNC—and with a $1 million discount from the competing offer as an act of goodwill for conservation. Fishbein spoke with grim reality: "If FleetBoston closed the deal with another group, it would be all over for us." We may never know the final reasons for FleetBoston's decision to negotiate with TNC for the sale of their debt. Clearly, concern about the bank's public image, struggles with the Chilean government over permits, Ed Crutchfield's relationship with FleetBoston's CEO, and TNC's agreement to raise its offer into a competitive range all played a part in the decision.

To hand over control, however, the bank would need to sell its debt to TNC and to help consolidate the remaining debt on the property. With $10 million in debt, FleetBoston held the largest share of the assets but two Chilean banks had $6 million in additional debt as well. To protect their assets, TNC and FleetBoston needed the first mortgage on the property to be held by a single entity. This consolidation would reduce dramatically the potential for something to go wrong in the bankruptcy proceedings. True to his word, Ward, on behalf of FleetBoston, worked quickly to tie up the loose ownership ends and passed these along to TNC, at FleetBoston's cost. In the end, TNC purchased all of the bank notes, which had a face value of $16 million, for only $6.3 million.

In Chile, coordination amongst the conservation groups supported TNC's efforts to do the deal. David Tecklin at World Wildlife Fund in Chile coordinated support for the purchase with local Chilean groups. Francisco Solís (now TNC's project manager) acted as independent legal counsel for a Chilean conservation organization that decided to buy a small creditor's debt in order to be able to participate in the creditors' committee meetings and more closely track the bankruptcy proceedings.

The saga was not over yet, however, for although TNC now owned all of the notes and the mortgage on the property, the bankruptcy process had to still play out. Carlos Fernandez, working with an army of the best Chilean lawyers, spent several intense weeks navigating the rapids of the Chilean bankruptcy process to avoid any surprise claims or law suits by other creditors. On November 4, 2003, the auction was held and much to our relief, no other bidders showed up to challenge TNC's offer. In order to obtain clear title, TNC ultimately shelled out an additional $1 million to pay other minor creditors but the $7.3 million purchase was a great victory for conservation. At fifty dollars per acre, this was great conservation value for the money especially when compared to the price of land in the United States. And the property had been appraised at $7.5 to $10 million.

Having used the power of the bankruptcy court to acquire the property at a favorable price, TNC now faces the daunting prospect of repaying its loan from TNC's revolving land protection fund. The global significance of the temperate coastal rainforest, and TNC's ability to respond adeptly to this opportunity quickly attracted funding commitments from World Wildlife Fund ($1 million) and the Global Conservation Fund of Conservation International ($750,000). With a hefty funding still needed for the purchase and long-term management, creative thinking is adding yet another wrinkle to this transaction. Fast-growing eucalyptus had already been planted on nine thousand acres of cleared land. That is a lot of work and expense. One alternative was to sell the timber rights to raise and harvest these trees, with the final clear-cut to be restored with a mix of native species. A local company that had watched the bankruptcy proceedings closely was indeed interested. In the end TNC made the decision that hiring contractors to do the harvesting would allow greater flexibility in managing this fragile terrain and ultimately yield greater value than selling the timber rights up front. One third of the plantations are now ready to harvest and the rest within eight to ten years. Together these harvests could provide upwards of $5 million toward the project's ultimate cost, while adhering to strict harvesting standards that ensure the protection of the soil and watersheds, and provide jobs for the local communities.

In assessing the deal some months later, Greg Fishbein reminded us yet again, "If we had risked letting the deal go to bankruptcy court in the hopes of winning a cheap bid, we would have been sadly disappointed." It's clear that FleetBoston and the other banks wanted a controlled disposition and would have cut a deal with another party if not us to avoid an unpleasant surprise in court. Bankruptcy in another country can be a nerve-racking experience but in the end, the rewards of obtaining this property for conservation made the investment worthwhile.

Dealing with foreclosures and bankruptcy is a high-risk and high-reward Wall Street business. Coincidentally, another defaulted company was simultaneously struggling for survival in Chile—this time the Trillium Corporation's Rio Condor project in Tierra del Fuego. The eight hundred and fifty thousand acres, bought with great fanfare in the early 1990s by Trillium's colorful and controversial president and founder, David Syre, and touted as the first "sustainably managed natural forest business" in Chile, had run into controversy from the very beginning. The area, comprising thousands of acres on the Straits of Magellan straddling Argentina and

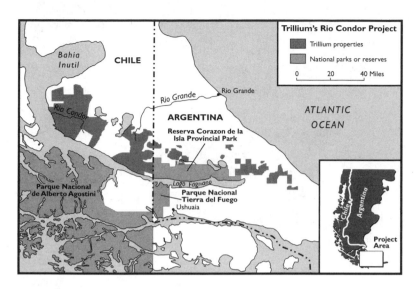

Figure 3.2

Trillium's Rio Condor Project

Chile, represented some of the only southern beach forests in the world. Furthermore, it had never been harvested. Despite the methodical and enlightened efforts of a team of forest consultants, well documented in David Lindenmayer and Jerry Franklin's book, *Conserving Forest Biodiversity*, the project ran into political and economic snags that ultimately led to its default on $30 million in notes owed to investors and lenders.[1]

The fine art of buying defaulted notes occupies a special realm in the investment banking business and is played only by big and strong investment banks, such as Goldman Sachs, Morgan Stanley, and a handful of others. In 2004, Goldman devoted an astonishing $5.7 billion dollars to this business. In February of 2002, Goldman acquired a portfolio of distressed debt from Capital Consultants, a financial company in the United States in liquidation. Within that portfolio was a package of delinquent notes of the Trillium Corporation and related entities that were secured by the forestland in Chile as well as a sawmill in Punta Arenas, Chile, and additional forest property in Argentina. Although Goldman never publicly admitted it, they clearly purchased the Trillium notes for a fraction of face value. Many investment bankers would not have recognized the ecological value of these lands but fortunately Hank Paulson, Goldman's conservation-minded chairman did. He posed a question to TNC's management: "Would TNC be interested in helping Goldman understand the full value, including conservation resources of this 850,000 acres?" In short order some of TNC's best legal, contractual, and conservation experts were in Chile trying to understand the vast landscape being acquired by Goldman. Phil Tabas and Dennis Wolkoff, both lawyers in TNC's Boston's office and among the best conservation deal makers in TNC's history, were paired with Josh Royte and Robin Cox, conservation planners working out of the Maine and California field offices. Together they would develop a conservation plan that could be part of Goldman's calculus in determining the fate of the land. In the end, after looking at the extraordinary ecological value and the vastness of this wilderness area, Goldman made a historic press announcement. They intended to give the property to an international conservation organization for stewardship as soon as they perfected their ownership through the foreclosure proceedings. In making the announcement they declared, "Goldman Sachs did not originally intend to acquire this land. But having acquired the notes secured by the properties, it explored a number of options to monetize both the notes and the properties secured by the notes including the sale of the land. But on further analysis, given the unspoiled nature of the tract of the land, the Firm determined that this was a unique opportunity to permit the ecologically important key features of the land to be conserved for the future, reflecting the viewpoint of the Firm's senior management."[2] Goldman also indicated that they would take a deduction for its contribution against its U.S. taxes as one way to make sure they gave a partial return to their shareholders. The key conservation planning work TNC's staff had put into mapping the area and assessing its ecological value had paid off in a big way.

The next step was to get David Syre on board. A court fight on fore-closure and default issues would add delays and needless expense to the project. At first, Syre was resistant but the reality of his situation brought him to the table for a new deal. He would surrender his interest in all the land in Chile but retain harvesting rights and an option to buy back his ownership in Argentina within two years. This cleared the way for Gold-man to take control of the property.

Ultimately a Chilean conservation group is probably the right man-ager for these important assets but in the meantime, Goldman has an-nounced that it is giving the land to the venerable Wildlife Conservation Society. Early on TNC and Goldman had concluded that because Hank Paulson serves as chair of both organization's boards, a deal with TNC in-volving a charitable contribution of this magnitude would be inappro-priate. Nonetheless, TNC and other conservation groups will need to be proactive in implementing the conservation vision that is emerging as the highest and best use for this property. The prospect of setting aside such a large portion of their landscape by outside groups has local communi-ties and the governments on guard and their support for a new future for the landscape will be critical to achieving success.

Conservation investment banking is an emerging new field. Skilled practitioners with experience in both conservation and business can lever-age successful conservation out of the failed investments and loans of oth-ers. If businesses can use these skills to obtain value for their shareholders, why not conservation organizations? In the Valdivian coast project, it was TNC staff that developed and implemented the buyout of the failed com-pany. In the case of the Rio Condor project, one of the world's premier in-vestment banking companies did the heavy work of developing the final business plan for this property. In both cases, though, magnificent con-servation results at a huge scale were obtained by using the tools of busi-ness.

Box 3.1

Conservation Investment Banking

Like our earlier story about Great Northern and the Katahdin Project, these two triumphs for conservation in Chile show that an understanding of the banking and legal systems offers new opportunities for conservation outcomes. The key lessons from these stories are:

Control the deal. Use public and political knowledge combined with legal and financial help to find a way to gain advantage in the transaction regardless of whether the process results in an auction, bid, or bankruptcy proceeding.

Future success will require an investment in new skills for land trust staff and through board memberships to guide these new style conservation tactics.

We have not seen the last of the hard financial times in the timber and farming sectors that control much of the land that conservation groups worldwide wish to protect. Even in good economic times businesses make mistakes, and this reality will continue to create negotiation opportunities for business and conservation groups.

4

Investing with an Attitude

People grow the food that people eat. People produce the lumber that people
use. People care properly or improperly for the forests and farms that are the
sources of those goods. People are necessary at both ends.

—Wendell Berry (Speech to Organic Groups, 1998)

In 1999, the fishing industry in the Gulf of Maine was in the midst of
struggling for its survival. The livelihood that had supported many towns
and generations of families faced unprecedented challenges. Federal regulators were considering rules that would effectively close down some fisheries, and public concern about the sustainability of marine-related
businesses along the Maine coast was increasing. Elizabeth Sheehan, fisheries project director at Coastal Enterprises, Inc. (CEI), faced a serious
dilemma. How could CEI continue to loan money for fishing boats and
marine businesses? Withdrawal of their support, with a history of funding over $11 million in 169 marine-related businesses, would be a crip-
pling blow for the already fragile marine business along the coast.

After twenty years as a leading community development nonprofit
corporation, CEI takes it mission seriously. As Elizabeth points out, "We
focus on the triple 'E' bottom line—positive impacts on the economy and
environment, while providing equity for disadvantaged people. If a loan
or investment is going to undermine the marine environment, we just

can't do it." As Elizabeth relates the story, "We were feeling pretty discouraged about the lack of real information to tell us if a proposed fishing loan was sustainable or not. Then it struck us, why not require the
boats as part of our loans to help support research to monitor the resource
being harvested." The idea of Fish Tags was born. For years economic development groups have used similar employment tags—"e" tags—to track
how many jobs are created by investments and loans but linking loans to
environmental and management concerns was a new idea. In the past CEI
had tried environmental screens to weed out problem loans but as Elizabeth explained, "After struggling with fifteen different measures of sustainability we realized that passive criteria did not get at the principal
problem, the lack of information. Fish Tags do."

Since that day in 1999, CEI has made $2.6 million in Fish Tag loans,
leveraging an additional $3.8 million in financing from others, and cre-
ating ninety-five new jobs. Fish Tags, linked to loans, have involved seventy fishermen and women in research projects that address a wide range
of industry problems. Eight projects have resulted in data that has been
directly incorporated into fishery management plans. The research provided new information on lobster, shrimp, red crab, horseshoe crab,
herring, whiting, and wild Atlantic salmon. One project looked at exper-
imental gear that demonstrated effective ways to reduce bycatch, thus allowing the state of Maine to open a limited commercial whiting fishery.
Several waste reduction efforts have ranged from installing more efficient
forklifts to new wastewater treatment systems. Fish Tags have even looked
at public health issues, focusing on monitoring mussels for paralytic shell-
fish poisoning ("red tide") and various other diseases.

The success of the Fish Tag program is making a difference in fishery
management and in the livelihoods of boat owners. Captain John
Williams of F/V Krystal James was the first participant in the Fish Tag program. Sheehan noted, "We thought that red crabs were an underutilized
resource but the last real study on the biomass had been done in 1977 and

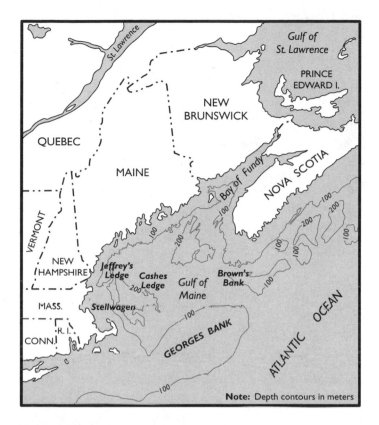

Figure 4.1
Map of the Fishing Grounds, Gulf of Maine

this was 1997, twenty years later." And Sheehan added, "We were nervous about funding new boats with such outdated biomass estimates." As a result, the red crab Fish Tag effort began. Captain Williams committed his company as part of his CEI loan to conducting unique monitoring, using electronic reporting to track size, sex, and water temperature data on the deep sea red crab population that he harvests. His boat is currently engaged with Darling Marine Center to reconduct the survey research for new biomass estimates. This information will feed into future management plans, providing real-time information for regulators and helping to determine whether harvest levels need to be adjusted.

In many cases CEI has been able to broker relationships between fishing boats and scientists working on research projects. Over twenty-one scientists from all of the top research institutions in New England are currently involved. Many of the fishing boats have found that supporting research projects, far from being a burden, has become an important supplemental income. As a result of Fish Tag projects, fishing boats have received over $360,000 of additional funding from government, foundations, and private researchers. Sheehan says this has been a winning partnership because it's expensive to get out on the ocean to collect good data.

The Fish Tag partnership is one successful example of linking investments to the long-term health and monitoring of an industry and it is part of a growing emphasis on socially responsible lending and investing. Marsha Glickman and Marjorie Kelly writing in *E Magazine* note, "Socially responsible investing (SRI) is something of a curious hybrid. Part capitalist outlet and part activist tool."[1] In just six years socially responsible investing has doubled to $2.164 trillion, and the shareholder advocacy activity has grown by 15 percent in the last three years alone. Activist groups sponsored 310 resolutions around social and environmental causes and although few of these resolutions actually pass, the percentage of shareholders voting for them has continued to climb.[2]

These funds have three core strategies to affect their social causes:

Screening favors investments based on social and/or environmental criteria as well as "buy lists" for those companies that are best in class on a range of social criteria, including the environment, employee relations, product manufacturing practices, and human rights issues.

Shareholder advocacy focuses on filing and voting on proxy resolutions. These efforts help move management in new directions by spotlighting

social concerns and corporate governance issues, often with the goal
of educating other shareholders about the companies' practices.
Community investing focuses on moving capital from investors down to the
community level, especially underserved populations, where there is an
urgent need to address housing, small-business growth, the environment, and community services, such as child care and health care.

CEI's work with Fish Tags is but one example of how targeted investing linked to environmental results can make a difference. Another example is the advocacy work of groups like the Rainforest Action Network
and the Dogwood Alliance, who use highly public campaigns to target
companies with questionable environmental records. These campaigns
include forcing resolutions on corporate practices, and they get results.
Recently Office Depot, under pressure from the Alliance, agreed to a wide-
ranging list of changes in procurement practices. The company offered to
support research and education activities aimed at increasing recycled
product use and ending sourcing of raw materials from endangered
ecosystems, such as Canada's boreal forest.

So how can land trusts benefit from this powerful investment energy?
Beyond the advocacy work, the concept of equity investments linked to
conservation may hold further promise. Back in the early 1980s, Lyme
Timber Company was a small forestland investment partnership. Strictly
by accident, as partner Peter Stein recounts, Lyme purchased a few properties with conservation attributes and soon found itself learning to work
with the National Forest and Park Services, state agencies, and conservation groups interested in acquiring pieces of their holdings. Stein recalls,
"Our first major deal was a leveraged buyout of a family-owned company
with mills and 180,000 acres of forestland. Lyme spun off the mills but
kept the land. Soon the Trust for Public Land and The Nature Conservancy
were knocking at Lyme's door wanting to buy property for conservation

purposes." At the time Stein was working for the Trust for Public Land (TPL) and took note of the potential in working with private companies on forestland deals. "But things didn't really start to heat up until TPL was negotiating to buy ten thousand acres of land from the old American Can Company. TPL could only afford the ten thousand acres but American Can/Primerica wanted to sell the entire ninety thousand acres, so I thought of Lyme Timber. Eventually Lyme bought the property and TPL got their land. A few years later I had the chance to work for Lyme and help them develop these interesting conservation-motivated transactions."

Since Stein joined the firm, every transaction done by the company has honored conservation as part of its purpose. Of sixty-five total projects, fifty have been timber deals where the unique blend of private capital and conservation interest has created a good investment for both.

In 2002 the company raised a new investment fund of $65 million to further its work in conservation-linked forest investments. "We could have raised $100 million if we wanted," says Stein. As it was, it took them only ninety days and nineteen thousand dollars to raise as much money as the group believes it could judiciously spend in the next three years. "We don't want to do plain vanilla deals—that's not our strength. We know conservation and forests. That's our business plan."

Conservation-minded investment funds have been tried with limited success by nonprofit groups, but Stein says that this business model is flawed. "Investors don't trust nonprofits to invest their money. We have a track record of delivering superior returns, and nonprofits don't have the investment skills. What they do have are good conservation skills so we partner with them on that and we analyze and manage the forest investment."

While Lyme does projects all over the United States, it admits its expertise is in the East. To be successful, Stein says you need local knowledge, good conservation partners, and a track record of delivering returns to investors. That means that Lyme will never be a billion-dollar fund, and there is plenty of room for other regional players with that combination of skills to carve out a business. Lyme is expanding to purchasing ranches in the West, where Stein says the same business model is applicable. "You can buy ranches in partnership with conservation, where easements and limited develop strategies keep the land intact and part of the working landscape. It is efficient financially for conservation because they are leveraging off our equity capital, and it's good for us because we are expanding our money with conservation capital."

Other groups are also looking at conservation-related forest investment funds. One such example is the efforts of John Tomlin, a former venture capitalist better known for his work in private equity with the Vista Group. Tomlin is now raising capital to invest in sustainable forestry ventures in partnership with conservation groups. Tomlin explains, "I was busy making a living as a venture capitalist and entrepreneur when my first child was born with serious health problems. I had to take time off from business and focus on family. This gave me a lot of time to think about what was important in life and what I wanted to do next." Along the way, Tomlin met Terry Anderson, the executive director of The Property and Environmental Research Center (PERC), a nonprofit that researches and advocates for market-based approaches to environmental and conservation problems. "I started to look around for business ideas where conservation and private capital markets could work together to solve problems in a win/win manner. This search led me to sustainable forestry as a great opportunity to test this concept."

With that in mind, Tomlin founded Conservation Forestry, LLC. Tomlin's idea is that Conservation Forestry will be the preeminent timberland investment fund manager for conservation-related forestry transactions. The concept is to create an investment management organization that aligns private equity with conservation capital for the purpose of acquiring and managing large forest landscapes. The investment fund would do so in a manner that maintains and enhances the conservation values of the forests while providing a competitive return to the private investors.

The acquisition would be a collaborative effort between private equity and conservation organizations to purchase timber properties. Tomlin notes, "This lowers the acquisition cost for private investors purchasing timber properties by monetizing the conservation values of the timberlands at the point of acquisition through a sale to the conservation partners. Therefore, the investment returns are based on sustainable timber cash flows instead of speculative development values in later years." This approach allows conservationists to take advantage of large-scale timberland transactions in which the costs of acquisition would have been prohibitive, either because of the scale of the deal or because a significant portion of the property has low conservation values. With the ability to bid together with Conservation Forestry, conservation groups can operate at a larger scale and still only commit the funds necessary to protect the conservation values they want. Conservation Forestry believes that its approach will lower risk to its investors because they will lock in payment for conservation values upfront and that they will benefit from access to attractive opportunities through the conservation community's deal network. Kent Gilges, one of The Nature Conservancy's forest program directors and a mover behind this concept, points out that "over the next decade there will be 15 to 30 million acres of timberlands changing hands as a result of the forest industry's restructuring and divestitures. This is a historic opportunity for conservation groups to dramatically increase their stake in the management of large areas of habitat currently supplying the fiber needs of the forest products industry. The challenge is that we need access to large sources of capital to take advantage of this opportunity."

Activist shareholders, socially conscious investors, and environmental advocacy groups are showing the power of investing with an attitude toward the environment. Ron Phillips, the president of CEI, calls this the "power of equity. By using capital investments, either through loans or equity investments, we are influencing all of the companies we work with, their competitors, and their customers." The $2.1 trillion invested in socially responsible investing is a lot of leverage if we can focus that investment energy. Lyme Timber, Fish Tags, and a host of other examples are pointing the way.

Box 4.1

Investing with an Attitude

Watchdog and Research Organizations

Coalition for Environmentally Responsible Economics (CERES)
Phone: 617-247-0700
Website: www.ceres.org

A coalition of environmental, investor, and advocacy groups that holds companies to a ten-point code of environmental conduct.

Social Investment Forum
Phone: 202-426-5270
Website: www.socialinvest.org

A nonprofit membership group for financial professionals promoting the practice and growth of socially responsible investing (SRI).

SRI Periodicals

Business Ethics
Website: www.business-ethics.com

The oldest and still-leading chronicler of the SRI industry.

GreenMoney Journal
Phone: 800-849-8751
www.greenmoneyjournal.com

Quarterly newsletter and excellent web site.   **continued**

Box 4.1 continued

Investment Funds and Managers

Coastal Enterprises, Inc.
36 Water Street
P. O. Box 268
Wiscasset, ME 04578-0268
Phone: 207-882-7552
Website:www.ceimaine.org

Lyme Timber
23 South Main
Hanover, NH 03755
Phone: 603-643-3300
Website: www.lymetimber.com

Conservation Forest Partners LLC
105 N. Second Street
Suite 233
Livingston, MT 59047
Phone: 406-222-9790
E-mail: JMTomlinMT@aol.com

Part II
Creating New Environmental Markets

5

Carbon and Forests

Without prices being set, Nature becomes like an all-you-can-eat buffet—and
I don't know anyone who doesn't overeat at the buffet.

—Richard Sandor (Quoted in Daily and Ellison *The New Economy of Nature*)

In the early 1990s, Dan Quinn and Hermes Justiniano, conservationists
working in Bolivia, struggled with an urgent threat to the future of Noel
Kempff Mercado National Park. Despite a decade of concerted work to
strengthen the park's management, persistent commercial logging around
the protected area continued to eat away at the critical buffers surrounding the park. Over 1.5 million acres of adjacent land was now endangered
by government granted logging concessions which, at the time, had few
controls on the harvest, and over five hundred kilometers of new roads
cut through the forest. Already the first harvest had "high graded" the
forests, stripping them of mahogany, and now a second harvest for lesser-
known native species was underway. In addition, land clearing for other
uses was anticipated to increase as settlements from nearby Santa Cruz
and across the border from Brazil continued to expand. As Dan Quinn put
it, "We could see the handwriting. Without a major effort today, the opportunity to expand the park to ecologically viable boundaries would be
lost forever." During the dry season, many of the park's bird and mammal
species depend on migrations to the lower, moister, commercial forest

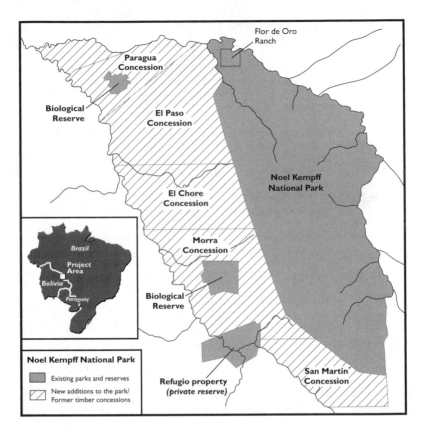

Figure 5.1

Noel Kempff National Park

areas. An expansion would add this valuable habitat and protect over sixty additional species of birds. However, there were significant monetary costs to halting the logging and bring the land into the national park. The government was collecting timber fees and hundreds of loggers were employed in the industry. Both would need to be compensated, but how to come up with the money? As Quinn observed, "Not only would it be expensive to buy out the logging concessions, the local communities feared a loss of jobs and urgently needed revenue to pay for health and educational services." Quinn and Justiniano's job would be daunting indeed.

With 130 million acres of forests, Bolivia has more tree cover than Central America and Mexico combined. Until recently, however, the country's forests were on their way to being severely degraded. With an average of nearly five hundred thousand acres per year being logged, the supply of high-value timber was less than a decade away from extinction. Noel Kempff was particularly vulnerable, with jaguars, giant river otters, and nine species of macaw all relying on intact forests and clean water for survival. Since those dark moments, a unique Carbon Mitigation project has breathed new life into conservation and sustainable management. The key to this concept was the recognition that by preventing commercial logging, substantial releases of carbon into the atmosphere would be prevented, offsetting emissions from other sources such as coal burning electric plants.

If it could be demonstrated that conserving forests reduced the amount of carbon released into the atmosphere then forest conservation might become a cornerstone in a global market whereby "credits" for reducing carbon emissions or sequestering carbon would be created. These credits could then be purchased by companies needing to reduce carbon emissions. This would create an efficient marketplace where the lowest cost alternatives for society as a whole would be selected by carbon emitters. To the extent preventing carbon losses to the atmosphere both enhanced conservation of forests along with addressing pressing climate change issues, a better outcome for all would be created.

The recognition that the environment is providing critical services to a healthy economy is a key new concept in the effort to engage business in conserving "natural capital," which, just like manufacturing or financial capital, provides a stream of benefits to society. As Brian Richter and Sandra Postel have observed, "To date, the economic benefits of ecosystem conservation have largely been ignored because most of nature's life-sustaining services are not valued in the marketplace. . . . As a result, we are prone to squandering the wealth of nature without ever tallying the losses."[1]

With an initial investment of $9.6 million in 1997, a consortium of investors, led by American Electric Power (AEP) and joined by PacifiCorp and British Petroleum (BP), supplied Justiniano's group, a Bolivian land trust called Fundación Amigos de la Naturaleza (FAN), with the resources to purchase and retire the logging rights on 1.5 million acres of forestland adjacent to the park—effectively doubling the park's size. The project expects to prevent the emission of 7 million tons of carbon (or over 25 million metric tons of carbon dioxide) during its thirty years. The stakes are high, for worldwide deforestation from logging contributes nearly 25 percent of annual carbon dioxide releases.

Even though the Kyoto Protocol has now been ratified, it seems unlikely that the carbon saved by this project will have an immediate market value because of the continued opposition of the United States government to the treaty, but E. Lynn Draper, American Electric Power's president and CEO at the time, saw the investment as a way for the company to prepare itself for carbon markets in the future. "We have developed cutting-edge technologies for accurately monitoring and verifying the carbon absorbed in the forest ecosystem. We hope our collaboration inspires similar initiatives from other organizations and helps inform the policy debate on this important issue."[2] Although none of the investors had significant business interests in Bolivia, the companies believed in the breathtaking conservation vision and wanted to have a seat at the negotiation table as carbon- and climate-related issues were debated in Congress and other forums.

In an economically challenging environment like Bolivia, the strategies to achieve real carbon mitigation have to extend beyond real-estate transactions. An endowment fund and a move to commercialize green products are only part of the effort to protect Noel Kempff Mercado National Park. Sustainable development also has to be one of the primary goals of the project. With a thousand people living along the park's border, defining a sustainable future for these residents is critical to the future of the park. FAN has hired approximately half of the park guards from the local communities, tapping into their knowledge of the area and their ability to explain conservation principles to other community members. In addition, the project has established revolving funds for microenterprises, such as heart-of-palm plantings and agroforestry projects. Most important, the project helped the local communities to attain legal status as indigenous peoples and to secure land tenure rights around their villages.

The Noel Kempff project has had other more indirect but tangible results in establishing and maintaining the conservation agenda in Bolivia. The credibility established in this project has resulted in a major new financial commitment from U.S. AID to launch a broader sustainable forest management project. Until recently, Bolivia's forests—which historically covered nearly one-half of the country—were being cut in a haphazard fashion. A small number of private companies monopolized the industry. Mahogany, oak, and cedar dominated nearly 90 percent of the timber trade. Companies coveted these marketable trees but in the process of extraction often damaged huge amounts of valuable but lesser known species that were left to rot in the forest. Roads gouged out to reach these preferred forests further strained the environment by contributing to erosion, water pollution, and unplanned settlements.

That devastation prompted the Bolivian government and U.S. AID to create the Bolivia Sustainable Forest Management Project (BOLFOR) in 1993. The first stage was successful enough that a second $15 million round of funding was approved in late 2003. In this new effort the focus is on creating a truly sustainable forest industry in which better harvesting practices and the utilization of lesser known species will increase the contribution of the forest industry to the economy while dramatically reducing the environmental damages caused by past practices.

A second example of conservation success inspired by the Noel Kempff project has been the signing of a National Implementation Support Partnership (NISP) agreement with the government of Bolivia. In

February 2004, at the Conference of Parties meeting under the Biodiversity Convention, the world's governments negotiated a Global Program of Action on Protected Areas. A consortium of international NGOs waged a year-long campaign to influence the outcome of these negotiations. For the first time, 188 governments have formally agreed to establish comprehensive, ecologically representative, and effectively managed and financed national and regional systems of protected areas—by 2010 for terrestrial systems and 2012 for marine systems.[3] Toward this overall objective, governments also committed to a broad set of ambitious and specific targets, timetables, and actions on protected areas within their countries.

The NGOs put forward a joint commitment to help governments spell out collaborative activities to be undertaken within the country to implement the Convention on Biodiversity. Bolivia was one of the first countries to agree to a formal memorandum, in part due to the positive and constructive role played by the successful carbon project.

In 2000, after the successes at Noel Kempff and similar projects in Belize and Brazil where over $30 million worth of carbon-motivated money had been invested, it seemed as though a new age of linking carbon mitigation to conservation was dawning. However, several factors have conspired to curtail the development of Noel Kempff-like projects. First, the failure of the United States, as the largest emitter of carbon in the world, to ratify the Kyoto Protocol has been a disincentive for other utilities, automobile manufacturers, and countries to invest in the marketplace. More importantly perhaps has been the difficulty in establishing forest conservation as an eligible activity under the Clean Development Mechanism (CDM) provisions of the treaty. CDM provisions were conceived to incentivize industries in developed countries to make carbon related investments to improve the economies of developing countries. So far, sequestering carbon through forest conservation has not been approved and many other promising CDM projects in other categories of carbon reduction are still struggling to get off the ground. It is thus not surprising that few new major carbon investments linked to conservation have materialized.

Despite the absence of official U.S. government support for Kyoto, the private sector is still pushing ahead with market mechanisms. The Chicago Climate Exchange (CCX) began trading carbon credits in late 2003, and with the rest of the world pressing ahead to implement carbon reductions through Kyoto, multi-national companies located in the U.S. are showing interest in the work of the Exchange. CCX creates a formal mechanism for companies to meet their legally binding reduction objectives through on-site emission reductions, allowance trading, and the limited number of offset projects approved through the CDM approach. One of the key potential barriers to trading has been the lack of standards for measuring companies' baseline emissions, monitoring compliance with reductions, and measuring offsets and reductions effectively. CCX has pioneered a comprehensive architecture of standards. With these mechanisms in place, carbon trading, while still small compared to the need, has nearly doubled in the last year and prices are rising as companies gain confidence in the market. So far, however, conservation projects are not part of the trading scheme because of the failure to approve forest conservation as part of the CDM approach.

New strategies are emerging in the United States, though, that could have profound financial implications for conservation projects. Inspired by early efforts in Oregon and Massachusetts, twenty-two states are considering or have adopted legislation on carbon sequestration, and a number of intergovernmental groups are pushing ahead with initiatives such as the Northeastern Regional Greenhouse Gas Initiative. This new strategy of developing regional and local initiatives is good news for conservation groups. One theory is that companies trying to negotiate through the maze of varying state programs may begin calling for federal legislation. Bill Stanley, one of The Nature Conservancy's (TNC) carbon experts, explains, "If we can get a critical mass of states developing carbon markets on their own, sooner or later industry and the federal government will come to the conclusion that one national system makes more sense in the long run."

And states are taking up the challenge. California is one such example. The state has unveiled an ambitious plan to require automakers to cut emissions of carbon dioxide and other gases linked to global warming over the next decade. Although the plan will likely be challenged in court, the California plan requires manufactures to start reducing carbon dioxide emissions by 2009 with the aim of achieving a 30 percent reduction by 2015.[4]

In August 2003, nine northeastern states announced that they would develop a regional carbon trade program to reduce carbon dioxide emissions from power plants. The states are developing model rules for a regional cap in emissions and for a trade program that may include land-based carbon offsets, such as the Bolivia project. The project got underway when New York governor George E. Pataki sent letters to the eleven governors from Maine to Maryland, inviting their states' participation in developing a regional cap-and-trade program covering carbon dioxide emissions from power plants within two years. By July 2003, the governor had received positive responses from eight of those governors. After discussions got underway, representatives from the Eastern Canadian Provinces Secretariat and the Province of New Brunswick began observing the process.

The positive response from the governors should come as no surprise. All of the Northeast and Mid-Atlantic states are in various stages of studying or implementing programs to reduce greenhouse gas emissions. For example, in April 2000, New Jersey adopted a statewide goal of reducing greenhouse gas emissions to 3.5 percent below 1990 levels by 2005. Similarly, the New England governors and the Eastern Canadian premiers issued a Climate Change Action Plan in August 2001, which calls for the reduction of greenhouse gases to 10 percent below 1990 levels by 2020. New York's State Energy Plan calls for the reduction of the state's carbon emissions to 5 percent below 1990 levels by 2010 and to 10 percent below those levels by 2020. The regional cap-and-trade program will assist all participating states in reaching specific goals.

Maine has been studying the issue of how proactive investment in the forest and agriculture sectors could contribute to the reduction of greenhouse gases in that state. Among the areas of potential intervention include:

Forestland protection. Even in rural Maine, forestland has been converted to urban land at a rate of 196,000 acres over fifteen years. This loss of cover results in substantial release of carbon to the atmosphere and a reduction in sequestration potential.

Increasing stocking with fast growing trees or plantation softwoods that absorb carbon faster than natural forests.

Early commercial thinning or lighter harvests to accelerate growth so that more carbon is accumulated at a faster rate.

Increasing harvest rotation length. Maine forest stands have decreased from an average age of sixty-eight years in 1982 to fifty-five years in 2003. This trend results in no carbon being emitted longer than rotation sequestration.

Not all of these have positive biodiversity or conservation values at the forest stand level and are likely to provoke considerable debate in the years ahead. For example, conversion of native stands to fast-growing plantations may increase carbon retention but substantially reduce wildlife habitat.

The savings compare favorably to Maine legislative targets for Greenhouse gas reductions of around 1 million metric tons of carbon dioxide per year.[5] None of these calculations yet speak to the cost of accomplishing these goals but show that many actions taken together can have a positive effect on the greenhouse gas problem facing even rural states like Maine.

The Midwest Forest Restoration Project demonstrates the potential of forestland restoration-based carbon strategies. Indiana soil once hosted 20 million aces of forest cover. After 150 years of agriculture, only two

Table 5.1

Maine Forestry Greenhouse Gas Savings

Avg. annual reductions year 2020 based on 100-year sequestration cycle	1000s of Metric Tons of CO_2 Emissions
Forestland protection	477.02
Increased stocking with fast growing trees	737.04
Early commercial thinning	282.39
More light harvests	3.31
Increased harvest rotation	(No consensus yet)
Total annual	1,521.51

(Source: Maine Greenhouse Action Plan, 2004.)

thousand acres of virgin forests remain intact. TNC began a program to focus on one of the most biologically diverse landscapes in the Midwest. The area encompasses rugged woodlands, prairie-opening waterfalls, giant promontories, and clear streams. The land attracted the eminent ecologist E. Lucy Braun in the late 1920s because the unique geography and underlying calcareous substrates created a distinct biological resource. But, with 90 percent of the forest converted to agricultural use, the concept of reestablishing native forests and restoring the ecosystem at an ecologically viable scale is a massive task. Thanks to an investment of five hundred thousand dollars from the Cinergy Corporation, those efforts are underway on a thousand acres of key ecological reserves. The goal is to plant 27,000 native trees along the riparian corridors and to expand, over time, old-growth areas, such as TNC's Indiana Big Walnut Nature Preserve. The designers hope to avoid or mitigate an estimated 150,000 tons of carbon releases. Although small compared to the 7 million tons promised in Noel Kempff, this project points the way toward deploying carbon-motivated investment capital for land conservation in the United States.

The Pacific Forest Trust (PFT), a land trust focusing on the future of forests along the west coast, has been pioneering U.S.-based carbon projects with its Forest Forever Fund, set up to "bank" forest-based carbon credits from private forestland in the Pacific Northwest. PFT has protected all of its carbon projects with conservation easements to ensure that carbon will be retained and conserved. At least one power company, Vermont's Green Mountain Energy Company, has purchased credits. The scientific basis for this project grew out of innovative research showing that carbon gains were nearly doubled by extending the rotation of Douglas fir stands from a typical forty years to ninety years, a requirement of the conservation easement over PFT's carbon projects.[6]

PFT has been working to reduce barriers to adoption of carbon sequestration projects in the United States such as the lack of a standard way of recording and monitoring credits. They have been spearheading the creation of the nonprofit California Climate Action Registry. Under this program California will be the first state in the nation with a scientifically credible, standardized, and practical system by which to inventory, monitor, and report forest carbon changes.[7]

Even with developing state and regional markets, designing forest projects will be a challenging business. Many forestland owners mistakenly believe that just owning forests will qualify them for carbon credits. While there is little doubt that all forests help maintain the carbon balance of the atmosphere, to qualify as a carbon sequestration project all of the current market systems focus on the concept of "additionality"—that is, carbon projects must move beyond business as usual. This effort may be easy to verify if you are planting new trees on land where none existed before, as in the Edge of Appalachia project. Demonstrating that changes in management practices on existing wood lots increase carbon retention will be much harder to prove, especially if continued harvesting is contemplated. Projects will thus need to implement a detailed monitoring system to track carbon saved, and incorporate easements or other permanent restrictions that legally enforce the carbon sequestration, as PFT did.

Overall the United States lost 11.5 million acres of existing forest to development between 1982 and 1997, and the average size of woodlots is declining as parcels become subdivided and developed. Since 1990, according to the PFT, the United States has stored less forest carbon each year. Because of the loss and unsustainable harvest of private forests, this trend is expected to continue at least until the year 2020.[8] With forest cover in the United States declining after a brief rebound in the middle part of the twentieth century, carbon sequestration projects may be one of the greatest hopes in saving forests for the future, by investing private capital in the environmental services provided by natural forests.

Box 5.1

Working on Forest Carbon Issues

While maintaining forests is critical for supporting the globe's carbon cycle, it is important to understand that carbon credits or investments must be focused on *creating new sources that absorb carbon*, such as planting trees or *preventing the clearing or conversion* of land from forests, as in Noel Kempff. Just because you own an existing woodlot does not mean that you will be able to go into the carbon trading business.

The Additionality Test:

Without this specific investment, the carbon sequestration potential of the land would be reduced, lost, or simply not created. Some examples of potentially qualifying projects:

New planting to create forests where they have been lost for some time. Prevention of the imminent loss of forestland to development or conversion. (If other government actions would have likely prevented this loss—zoning or regulations, for example—then you will be unlikely to be able to claim a carbon credit.)

Some projects where eligibility will be difficult to establish under most approaches:

Maintaining existing woodlots or forests where little threat to conversion exists. (Not likely because the carbon benefits already exist.)

Incrementally improving the management of forests. (These incremental improvements will have a low carbon value per acre, and will be difficult to measure and to get to sufficient scale to be worth the effort.)

If the project would have happened anyway through market forces—certification or federal or state funding is already available.

The Partner Test

Because there are very limited markets, old hands at these projects suggest having a partner lined up to purchase the credits is absolutely critical. Developing a speculative project could be a waste of time until markets mature. Go to your local utilities and other energy users first and propose a partnership around a concept.

Leakage

This question goes to the core of whether the carbon you are sequestering is a unique addition to the planet's carbon bank. If the forest conversion is just going to shift next door, arguably nothing really has been added. In the Noel Kempff project leakage was addressed by an agreement with the former timber concessionaires, who were obligated to report on what they did with the compensatory funds and to cooperate on sustainable forestry practices on their logging concessions outside the project area.

Permanence

Projects must demonstrate that they are long-lasting. One corroboration would be conservation easements on the property; another, ownership by a government or conservation agency.

Box 5.2

Resources for Carbon Projects

Global Climate Change Initiative, The Nature Conservancy
4245 N. Fairfax Drive, Suite 100
Arlington, Virginia USA 22203-1606
Phone: 703-841-7436
Email: climatechange@tnc.org
Website: http://nature.org/initiatives/climatechange/index.html

Pacific Forest Trust
415 Aviation Blvd., Suite A
Santa Rosa, CA 95403
Phone: 707-578-9950
Website: www.pacificforest.org

Winrock International
38 Winrock Drive, Morrilton, Arkansas 72110
Phone: 501-727-5435
Fax: 501-727-5242
1621 North Kent Street, Suite 1200
Arlington, Virginia 22209
Phone: 703-525-9430
Fax: 703-525-1744
A private, nonprofit organization with climate expertise.

Table 5.2

Sampling of State and Regional Efforts to Control Climate Change

Area NE and Mid Atlantic States

Status Northeast Regional Greenhouse Gas Initiative (created by the governors of ten states)

Description A multistate cap-and-trade program covering greenhouse gas (GHG) emissions. The program will initially be aimed at developing a program to reduce carbon dioxide emissions from power plants in participating states, while maintaining energy affordability and reliability and accommodating, to the extent feasible, the diversity in policies and programs in individual states. The goal is to have a program design agreement by April 2005 or sooner. After the cap-and-trade program for power plants is implemented, the states may consider expanding the program to other kinds of sources.

Area California

Status Senate Bill 812, approved by governor, September 7, 2002.

Description Requires the California Climate Action Registry to: (1) adopt procedures and protocols for the reporting and certification of greenhouse gas emission reductions resulting from a project or an action of a participant; (2) adopt procedures and protocols, for carbon stores and carbon dioxide emissions resulting from the conservation and conservation based management of native forest reservoirs in California; (3) adopt procedures and protocols for the reporting and certification of specified reductions in emissions of greenhouse gases.

Area California

Status Assembly Bill 1493 approved by governor July 22, 2002.

Description No later than January 1, 2005, the state board shall develop and adopt regulations that achieve the maximum feasible and cost-effective reduction of greenhouse gas emissions from motor vehicles. The regulations should apply only to the 2009 and subsequent model years.

Area Connecticut

Status Public Act 90-219 H.B. 5696 (1990)

Description Connecticut passed the first state global warming law to require specific actions for reducing carbon dioxide. The Act establishes a broad range of energy conservation measures and allows the Environmental Protection Commissioner, in connection with air discharge permits, to require trees or grass to be planted to offset carbon dioxide emitted into the atmosphere.

Table 5.2 (continued)

Area Idaho
Status Senate Bill 1379, signed by governor March 27, 2002
Description Creates the Carbon Sequestration Advisory Committee and the Carbon Sequestration Assessment Fund.

Area Maine
Status Legislative Document 87, Signed by governor, April 6, 2001
Description Requires the Department of Environmental Protection to create a voluntary registry of greenhouse gas emissions. Maine has committed under the auspices of the New England Governors/Eastern Canadian Premiers (NEG/ECP) to reducing GHGs to 10 percent below 1990 levels by 2010.

Area Massachusetts
Status DEP Regulation 310 CMR 7.29, rule issued April 23, 2001
Description Requires the six highest-polluting power plants in Massachusetts to meet overall emission limits for nitrogen oxide (1.5 lbs/MWh) and sulphur dioxide (3.0 lbs./MWh) by October 1, 2004 and begin immediate monitoring and reporting of mercury emissions. Plant operators may meet the standard either by increasing efficiency at the plant, or by purchasing credits from other carbon dioxide reduction programs approved by the DEP.

Area Minnesota
Status Division of Lands and Forestry Statute Section 88.82 (1999)
Description Minnesota Releaf program is established in the Department of Natural Resources to encourage, promote, and fund the planting, maintenance, and improvement of trees in this state to reduce atmospheric carbon dioxide levels and promote energy conservation.

Area Nebraska
Status Legislative Bill 957, enacted April 10, 2000
Description Created a Carbon Sequestration Advisory Committee to document and quantify reductions related to agricultural practices; to provide duties; and to create the Carbon Sequestration Assessment Cash Fund. Legislative intent was to enable to Nebraska farmers/ranchers to participate in a carbon market.

Table 5.2 (continued)

Area New Hampshire
Status House Bill 284, signed by governor, April 2002
Description Does not explicitly mention sequestration offsets but does leave room for sequestration through implementing regulations: "Affected sources may use carbon dioxide allowances from federal or regional trading and banking programs, or other programs, acceptable to the department, to comply with the carbon dioxide emissions cap . . . "

Area Oregon
Status House Bill 2200, signed by governor, effective January 2002
Description Establishes a program for creating forestry carbon offsets from nonfederal forestlands and requires the State Forester to develop a forestry carbon offset accounting system. The bill defines a forestry carbon offset and authorizes the State Forester to enter in to agreements with nonfederal forest landowners as a means to market, register, transfer or sell offsets on behalf of nonfederal landowners. Also allows the State Forester to market, register, transfer or sell offsets on behalf of Forest Resource Trust.

6

The Bank of Nature

"The land has got to be productive." I heard Warner Glenn, Bill Miller, and Ray Turner say at different times. By saying this they aren't just articulating an old-fashioned Christian view about man's domination over the creatures of the earth. They are arguing for what one neighbor calls "working wilderness." They are saying that unless there is some economic return to the land, there is no defense at all against the pressures of development, which are spiraling outward from nearly every city and small town in the West.

—Verlyn Klinkenborg ("Crossing Borders: Good News from The Badlands," *Audubon* Sept. 1995: 36–44)

In many parts of the western United States, grasslands are declining in productivity as invasive and noxious weeds displace native grasses; furthermore, tree and shrub growth is on the rise, the result of a century of fire suppression and overgrazing. In northern New Mexico, tree and shrub encroachment has reduced the grassy component of the landscape by 55 percent since 1935.[1] The change has not been limited to isolated areas, for all across the West studies show the increase of woody species at the expense of grass. The resulting shift has diminished the ecological diversity of the landscape and put significant economic pressure on the ranching community, for as the grass resource declines so must the viability of grazing cows. In the hot dry landscapes of the West it can take as much as fifteen thousand acres to graze a few hundred cows.[2] Even modest changes in grassland productivity can spell economic disaster, forcing the rancher away from grazing and toward development.

The mechanics of restoring grasslands are clear. Reintroduce controlled fire; clear accumulated woody debris; control invasive species; and apply more careful grazing practices. However, implementing these strategies without bankrupting the cattle industry is difficult. In restoration projects cattle are displaced for months as woody debris is cleared and grass is allowed to regrow, and even then it may take years of careful tending to establish historic conditions. Most ranchers have no place to put their cattle during these efforts even if they are prepared to undertake the work. Simply removing cattle forever is also not the answer. Without ranchers who are motivated to maintain and restore the landscape, invasive species often take over and it is unlikely that the historic grazers, buffalo and elk, now replaced by cattle in most of the West, will again become a vital ingredient in keeping the savanna clear except in modest special management areas.

Out of this dilemma, the concept of grassbanking was born. By providing an alternative place for cows to graze while restoration is undertaken, grassbanks give ranchers a practical solution to maintaining their herds during the restoration effort. Grassbanking began in 1994, the brainchild of Drum Hadley of the Animus Foundation in the Malpai borderlands of New Mexico. Local ranches swapped conservation easements on their ranches for grazing privileges on the foundation's 325,000-acre Grey Ranch. The Grey was first purchased by The Nature Conservancy (TNC) in the 1980s and is now owned by the local nonprofit foundation. The easements, equal in dollar value to the forage that the cattle consume on the grassbank, include provisions to protect the ranches from subdivision and other development, to restore riparian area, and to prepare lands for burning. This concept, trading something of monetary value to the grassbank owner in exchange for biodiversity protection, has now been applied

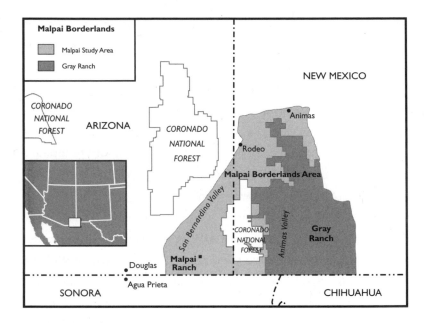

Figure 6.1

The Malpai Borderlands

on almost three hundred thousand acres of public, tribal, and privately owned ranch lands across the West.

The concept of grassbanking, though, goes far beyond the mere mechanics of restoration for it calls for a new way of thinking about community and future of ranches. The real issue at stake is the fate of open land and the economic justification for it. As William deBuys has observed, "In the West a small but growing movement claims that property rights are absolute, inviolable. The members of the Malpai Borderlands Group have decided for themselves that asserting absolute property rights will inevitably mean the destruction of the West, the disappearance of open land. They have found a series of shared possibilities. You use the Grass Bank only by ceding development rights to the Malpai Group. You derive the benefits of neighboring only by contributing to the common good, not by vigilantly defending what you call your own."[3]

At least eight grassbanks are underway, and the possibility of leveraging conservation beyond the borders of a protected area is attracting a lot of interest. As Lynda Poole, who manages TNC's sixty-thousand-acre Matador Ranch in Montana, explains, "You could lock up the land that we own here, say it was only for species preservation, and you would have an impact on 60,000 acres. You would also isolate yourself from your neighbors and create distrust." She adds, "But with Grassbank, you create a working relationship with your neighbors, and you spread the conservation impact over a large enough area that you start to see benefits on a landscape scale, not just on an island."[4] On the Matador, neighboring ranchers who are protecting endangered species and habitat receive a discount on grazing costs. The black-footed ferret, the most endangered mammal in the United States, as well as other rare species, such as the swift fox and the mountain plover, need special management. Ranchers who participate in this protective effort receive discounted grazing rights on TNC's land. One participating rancher, for example, owns nearly eight hundred acres of prairie dog town. TNC's researchers calculated how much forage the prairie dogs consumed, and the rancher was given an equivalent reduction in his grazing fees. All thirteen ranchers participating in the plan receive a discount to pay for weed control programs, and they agree not to convert any of the grasslands to croplands.[5]

The economics of grassbanks are interesting because the modest revenue generates such significant conservation. The Heart Mountain Grassbank of TNC's Wyoming chapter is a case in point. Located on the eastern edge of the greater Yellowstone ecosystem, it is modest in size, with fifteen thousand acres providing grass to feed 2,000 and 3,100 cows per month. TNC bought the ranch for about $1 million, to protect it from development. The market rate for renting pasture in the area is about twenty-five dollars per month per cow. The Conservancy charges eight dollars per cow, and the participants contribute the difference of seventeen dollars in conservation. Usually this commitment is "paid" by the ranch's own work

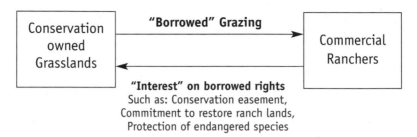

Figure 6.2

How Grassbanks Work

to restore grazing areas by removing woody plants and reintroducing fire. All totaled, the costs of running the grassbank are a modest seventy to eighty thousand dollars per year, with ranchers paying about seventeen thousand of that amount in grazing fees and the balance provided in conservation work. Heart Mountain works closely with Shoshone National Forest, where most of the grazing allotments managed by local ranchers are located. The ten-year projection shows that by providing alternative grazing ground for ranchers the grassbank will help restore ecological health to 115,000 acres of public lands and 55,000 acres of private lands. The grand total of 170,000 acres leverages Heart Mountain's own 15,000 acres by more than tenfold—all on a budget of eighty thousand dollars per year. An excellent return on a modest conservation investment.[6]

Water is another form of currency in the arid West. For more than a hundred years, ranchers, power generators, and towns and cities have jealously guarded their water rights. What's new is that over the last two decades conservation has emerged as a major influence in water disputes, and an emerging tool of choice is to apply market-based water-trading systems. The first major water transaction motivated by conservation helped settle a long-running, acrimonious dispute over the water from California's Mono Lake. In 1983, under the public trust doctrine, the Environmental Defense Fund, National Audubon Society, and other

Box 6.1

Model Grassbanking Projects

Gray Ranch, Southwestern New Mexico

The Malpai Borderlands Group implemented the first grassbank in 1994 on this 502-square-mile property originally purchased by TNC and now owned by a partner organization. Forage is traded for conservation easements and improvements on the ranches owned by members of the grassbank.

Valle Grande, New Mexico

Established by the Conservation Fund in 1998, this grassbank consists of 240 acres of private property and 36,000 acres of forest service grazing allotments. Local ranchers receive forage in exchange for conducting pre-scribed burns, thinning forestland, and restoring streams.

Heart Mountain Ranch, Cody, Wyoming

With forage scarce in this area, the Heart plays a key role in supporting native grassland preservation and habitat restoration for sage grouse, elk, and other species, The six hundred acres of lowland pasture provide grazing to six ranchers while they conduct restoration projects on their lands and grazing allotments.

Sun River, Augusts, Montana

TNC's 380 acres of private-land grassbank along the Sun River Basin began in 2001. Local ranchers hope to use the model to develop a collective grassbank comprising small parcels of grassland donated by nonranching owners. These landowners trade forage in exchange for cash, weed control, and trespass prevention while TNC protects biodiversity on the ranches.

continued

Box 6.1 continued

Vina Plains Preserve, Lassen Foothills, California

The 4,600-acre Vina Plains Preserve was converted into a grassbank in 2002. It offered reduced rates on grazing to local ranchers who conducted prescribed burns and other invasive weed control measures on their lands.

Matador Ranch, Malta, Montana

This ranch includes thirty-one thousand deeded acres and twenty-nine thousand acres of state and federal leased lands. Begun in 2003, the grassbank offers ranchers reduced grazing rates in exchange for weed control, preservation of grassland, and habitat protection.

Juniper Hills Preserve, Prineville, Oregon

TNC's Juniper Hills Preserve holds a grazing permit for 6,879 acres on the Ochoco National Forest. The permit will provide a grassbank to local ranchers while their own allotments on Forest Service and BLM lands are improved by prescribed burns, streamside fencing, and weed control. It was the first grassbank in the Pacific Northwest.

Adapted from Stephanie Gripne and Hal Herring, "Model Grassbanking Projects," *Nature Conservancy Magazine* (Spring 2004): 21. Used with permission of Hal Herring.

environmental groups sued the state of California, demanding that Los Angles reduce withdrawals from the lake. Reduced water levels threatened the lake's sensitive ecosystem. Legal issues notwithstanding, the water problems of Los Angles were real and begged for resolution. Creative thinking provided a solution: with Los Angles and similar cities paying over $250 per acre-foot of water and farmers paying as little as $10 for the same quantity, the opportunity for a marketplace was real. A farmer selling water from the Central Valley to Los Angles could reap a substantial

return, which could be invested in labor- and water-saving irrigation systems that offset the loss of water from the farmer's fields. A market-based
system could actually supply Los Angles with the water it needed while reducing dependence on critical ecosystems like Mono.

The problem, though, was that Los Angeles was addicted to cheaper
water from Mono Lake, and the city strongly opposed the costs of purchasing water rights. It took five more years for the Mono Lake situation
to be resolved. Water trades were part of the ultimate solution, although
not from farmers as had been proposed, but from a variety of federal and
state projects, where investments in waste water reclamation provided the
necessary water volumes.[7]

The next advance in using water markets for conservation came in
western Nevada, where a federal irrigation project was wreaking havoc in
the critical wetlands around the Stillwater National Wildlife Refuge outside a rapidly growing Reno. Irrigation was increasing; water diversions
were escalating; and the wetlands began to dry up. Once covering one
hundred thousand acres, the wetlands were down to seven thousand acres
in the early 1990s. The once pristine area had become heavily polluted
with trace mineral elements leaching out of the soil, and all manner of
agricultural pesticides, herbicides, and fertilizers. In 1987, 7 million fish
died, and waterfowl populations dropped to 40 percent of historic levels.
As David Livermore, director of TNC's Great Basin office at the time observed, "this was not a case where you could go out and buy 40 acres in the
middle of Stillwater in an effort to save the marsh. That would have been
like sticking our heads in the sand."[8]

Inspired by work on water markets, TNC's Great Basin office came up
with an approach that ultimately turned environmental tragedy into one
of the most interesting case studies of water trading for conservation. In
1993, TNC set a goal of retiring twenty thousand acre-feet of water use by
buying up allotments from farmers. Within a year it had purchased fourteen thousand acre-feet of water in part through $1.5 million in private

donations. With this success the State of Nevada, now with a larger war chest, joined forces with TNC and the U.S. Fish and Wildlife Service. As the concept gained momentum, the partners developed criteria for selecting water rights to buy and developed an auction system to efficiently price water rights. With a ready market for water in place, ranchers and farmers began to think about calculating the benefits of selling water rights compared with the costs of improving water utilization efficiency.

The public value of water rights is now becoming evident in the use of water for energy generation. For hundreds of years companies built dams to convert rivers and lakes into sources of privately owned energy. In many cases, though, the water is actually owned by a public and the public has not historically been compensated for the use of those rights. Through the process of relicensing dams across the country, under the auspices of the Federal Energy Regulatory Commission (FERC), these rights are being reclaimed, often with conservation payouts. In Tennessee, Alcoa, the world's largest aluminum producer, entered into a deal on a dam owned by the company since 1913. Under the plan, the Great Smoky National Park will receive 186 acres of "biologically sensitive lands" by giving up 100 acres of already flooded lands currently in the park. In addition, Alcoa will give TNC an easement on six thousand acres of land plus an option for TNC to buy the land outright for the park. Similar deals have been struck in many other places across the country. Public interest in water rights is finally receiving some compensation through conservation commitments from energy generators.[9]

With the encouraging examples of waterbanks and grassbanks working in the West, TNC's Greg Low and Bill Weeks wanted to develop a similar concept for the thousands of small forest woodlots that dominate many of the eastern coastal states. Much of this land was former farmland, now reverted to forestland, but retaining its small-lot ownership. In many areas TNC faced a continuing loss of forest lots to development. Massive losses would continue if expensive real-estate purchases remained the only conservation option. Weeks and Low reasoned that many small-woodlot owners, caught in desperate financial straits, were being forced to sell land to developers. Cash flow from forest operations was irregular, often inadequate to pay taxes and manage the land with required annual investments. With a typical ten to twenty year period between harvests in the temperate forests of eastern United States, landowners were harvesting the land and then putting it up for development, because twenty years before the next round of income was just too long to wait. The concept was simple: if enough landowners "deposited" their land in a forestbank, the collective harvesting schedule of these lands would guarantee each landowner a dividend each year, in accordance with the amount of timber deposited in the bank.

Implementing forestbanks has proved more challenging than initially thought. Landowners have been reluctant to give up forestland for a regular dividend, in part because the returns from growing trees are small on these forty to one-hundred-acre forest lots and also because most of these landowners look to their wood lots for multiple uses—hunting and recreation, for example. A small regular dividend is not enough to motivate giving up some of these interests. However, as the concept has evolved, new ideas about forestbanks are gaining some traction. In the Clinch Valley of Virginia, TNC has struck a leadership deal with Stuart Land and Cattle Company, a family-owned company with seventeen thousand total acres, including substantial forestlands. This region of the country is a critical area for TNC where its program focuses on aquatic targets like globally rare freshwater mussels. Poor management practices, including logging and road construction on steep slopes, was leading to water quality problems. Under the terms of the initial deal, TNC will receive a forest management easement on 5,750 acres of prime forestland. In turn TNC will make annual "dividend" payments to the Stuarts, based on the timber inventory of the property. Over time TNC will harvest timber to generate revenues that will offset the annual payments. If the value of the timber

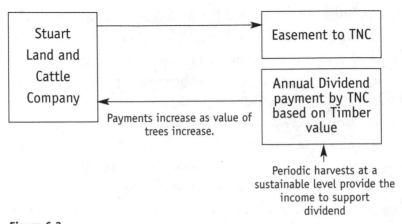

Figure 6.3
Clinch River Timber Bank

increases, the dividends will increase. The "capital" of trees will be reevaluated every ten years to set the new basis for paying dividends.

The landowners benefited from this structure because they now received regular income from the land but continued to own the underlying land. TNC benefited because it obtained a forest management easement that ensures the sustainable management of the property, but it did not have to pay for the easement in one lump sum. The annual payments are partially offset by periodic timber harvesting. With this first transaction under its belt, TNC's Virginia program is looking to add adjacent landowners to the project. With the positive experience of the first deal, Stuart has added an additional 4,000 acres to the project recently and a nearby landowner has put 1,800 acres into the program with a commitment of an additional 8,500 acres of forestland as soon as TNC can raise the funds required.

Nature's capital—water, grass, trees—is providing a unique opportunity. Although the concepts vary because no two landowners are the same and the needs of ranchers, farmers, and foresters are not identical, the "Bank of Nature" is opening new doors to saving this fragile earth. The

Bank's capital is land and its corresponding ability to grow products. The Bank's customers are landowners who are committed to the sustainable management of the landscape. Interest payments are in the form of conservation. Very simply, the concept works, and it demonstrates an exciting method for achieving conservation by working with the tools of business.

Box 6.2

Resources for the Bank of Nature

Grassbanking

An excellent resource of materials on grassbanking is maintained by Stephanie Gripne of Compatible Ventures LLC. See them at www. compatibleventures.com

Forest Banks

Clinch Valley Program
146 East Main Street
Abingdon, VA 24210
Phone: 276-676-2209

Water Banks and Water Trading Issues

Environmental Defense Fund
257 Park Avenue South
New York, NY 10010
Phone: 212-505-2100
Fax: (212) 505-2375
Website: www.environmentaldefense.org

Part III
Incentives

7

Greening Business

The question is, can we create profitable, expandable companies that do not destroy directly or indirectly, the world around them?

—Paul Hawkins

In the southeast Asian islands of Sumatra and Borneo, the survival of the world's orangutan population hangs in the balance. On these islands orangutans can still be found in the wild. Despite the orangutan's protected status, experts predict that the threats of uncontrolled logging, illegal poaching, and general environmental degradation mean that in all likelihood wild orangutans will be extinct by the year 2020.

One of the focus areas for orangutan protection is in East Kalimantan on the island of Borneo, part of Indonesia. Searching for these elusive great apes, researchers recruited and trained local villagers, and then began carefully surveying the remote and difficult lowland forest terrain found in the East Kalimantan. After nearly four rigorous months in the forest, the survey team stumbled on a large, previously unknown population of orangutans. Around 1,600 resting and "nesting" sites were counted—evidence of at least a thousand orangutans residing within a 345,000-acre area. This find may represent up to 10 percent of the world's estimated remaining wild orangutan population. "This group could be one of the three largest populations in the world," says Linda Engstrom, one of the field researchers.

The key to survival of these and other orangutan populations will be to retain these critical forests and protect them from unsustainable logging and the conversion to agriculture. In Indonesia this will be a major challenge. As Nigel Sizer, Director of The Nature Conservancy's Forest Conservation program in Jakarta, tells the story, "Every second a cubic meter of wood is stolen from Indonesia's forests—that's 50 million cubic meters this year alone! And that's not all. Every minute, the government loses $1,300 of tax revenue from this wood." That's over $670 million in lost tax revenue a year for Indonesia. Thirty million Indonesians depend on traditional subsistence activities in the forest. The destruction of vast areas of forest and the disruption of whole ecosystems threatens not only the orangutans but the existence of these people as well.

As Sizer points out, "There is not just one factor that is leading to this wholesale slaughter of the Indonesian forests; it's a combination of weak governance, poor law enforcement, ill-advised government policies, and lack of alternative income opportunities for rural poor. A particular problem for Indonesia and other similar countries is that the buyers have no way of knowing if a log on a loading dock is illegally harvested or not. And many buyers simply don't care."[1]

With Indonesia losing 56 million of its 345 million acres of forestland in the last decade alone, TNC and its partners are struggling to implement strategies that can be successful before it's too late. Sizer's strategy for saving the forests is based firmly in the market and financial sectors of the country. "Dealing with poverty and weak government is essential in the long run but we don't have decades, we have a few precious years. That's why our alliance between TNC and WWF is focused on drying up the demand for illegally harvested logs in the importing countries, such as Japan and China, and promoting responsible financing for forest-based business."

Some small successes have been achieved already. With the country historically linked to Holland, Dutch financial institutions are key investors in Indonesia's economy. In a major breakthrough, three of four major Dutch banks, under pressure from green groups in Europe, have agreed to stop funding oil-palm projects that are located on land cleared within the past five years. Many of the rampant fires and uncontrolled clearing of forest were thinly disguised efforts to prepare land for agriculture, especially the oil palm, an emerging source of cooking oil throughout the world. It is hoped that ending funding from the Dutch banks will curtail efforts to clear the forests. But even more tools will be needed. Sizer's group has launched a project to reduce illegal logging by marking legitimately harvested timber with bar codes. With proper labels, buyers in Japan or China can know for certain that the logs they purchase were harvested legally.

A four hundred thousand dollar pilot project in 2003 targeted the key orangutan areas, and TNC enlisted two Indonesian logging firms—Sumalindo Lestari Jaya and Daisy—to participate in the trial run. Under the new system, timber from logging companies adopting environmentally sound principles is bar coded, enabling it to be tracked from the cutting phase through shipping and delivery. Companies participating in the project must open themselves up to a rigorous audit by third-party inspectors from agencies such as the Switzerland-based Société Générale de Surveillance. Firms are evaluated according to seven corporate responsibility/environmental sustainability principles, including the environmental impact of their logging operations, adherence to Indonesian timber harvesting laws, and respect for workers' rights.

For the project to succeed, wood buyers in major importing countries must agree to buy only the properly labeled logs. Large buyers of Indonesian wood in the United States, including Home Depot, Inc. and Lowe's Companies, Inc., have already signed on to the program, guaranteeing an initial market for these certified timber exports.

By 2005, TNC hopes to have a dozen or so companies actively using the system, as well as a series of buyers lined up. The challenge is corruption at the local level and weak enforcement of existing Indonesian law.

"We can make a difference in some parts of the country with some companies, so we're focusing on areas that are significant in conservation terms or particularly environmentally sensitive," Sizer said. "While there are some segments of the private sector that are very difficult to work with, many powerful players want to see a change in forest management practices and exercise corporate responsibility," he added. "Whether companies will continue depends on the signals they get from the international market."[2]

Market pressures to be green are also having far-reaching impacts on Canada's forests. Canada's boreal region is one of the largest remaining unspoiled forests on earth. Its 529 million hectares (1.3 billion acres) harbor an abundance of Canada's signature wildlife, vast freshwater resources, some of the world's richest deposits of natural resources, and more than 4 million people, including many First Nations.

In a historic pact, key industry leaders joined with Canadian conservationists to create the Boreal Forest Conservation Framework. Among the first to sign were Domtar, Inc., the giant Quebec-based paper company that manages 22 million acres of forestland in Canada and the United States; Tembec, with fifty-five mills in Canada; and Suncor Energy, whose four thousand employees rank it as one of the largest players in the boreal zone. The framework is twofold: it calls for the establishment of a network of large interconnected protected areas covering about half of the country's boreal region, and it makes use of leading-edge, sustainable development practices in the remaining areas, including certification for forest practices. Gary Stewart, director for Ducks Unlimited conservation program in the boreal areas, observed, "This is a significant endorsement of the paradigm shift toward conservation that is currently underway in Canada's boreal forest."

These companies joined this effort for solid business reasons. In adjacent British Columbia, industry has watched the debate among First Nations, government, business, and environmental activists bring harvesting

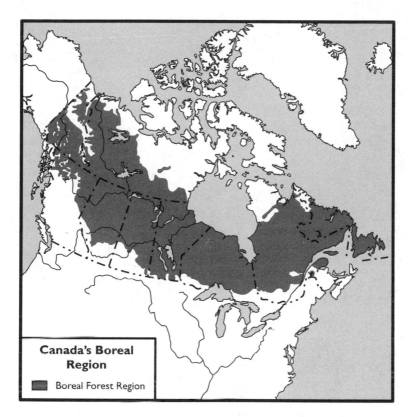

Figure 7.1
Canada's Boreal Zone

to a standstill along much of the rich temperate coast. The bitter ten-year
controversy has dramatically affected the industry's "social license" to operate. Raymond Royer, president of Domtar, told me, "We need to demonstrate to our customers that we are managing our forest sustainably. If they
are not convinced of our efforts, we will not be able to continue to do business. It's that simple."

The controversy in British Columbia has been focused in an area
known as the Great Bear Rainforest between the northern tip of Vancouver Island and the Alaska panhandle. This 21 million acre region of coastal

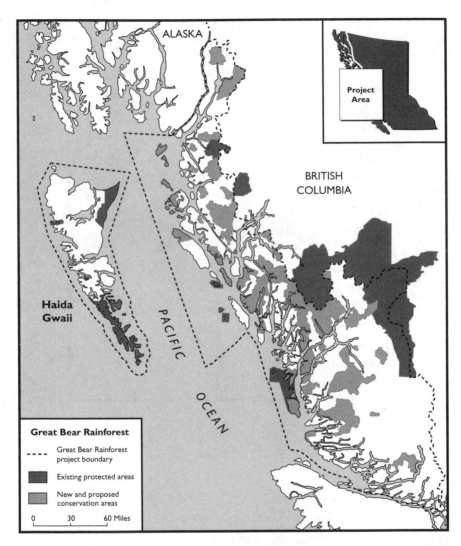

Figure 7.2

Great Bear Rainforest

temperate rainforests makes up a full quarter of what remains on the planet. The area is named for the unique and elusive bear known as the Kermode by First Nation people in the region. The Kermode is a creamy white variety of the black bear that numbers less than four hundred and is found only here. In the mid-1990s an intense global campaign was launched by activist groups targeting the trade and investment of the logging companies that were linked to the clear-cut logging of old-growth and the destruction of the forest. As a result, dozens of companies including Home Depot, the world's largest lumber store, and IKEA, the world's largest furniture retailer, joined the effort to reform logging in the region. These alliances ultimately resulted in an historic consensus agreement in 2001 signed by environmental groups, logging companies, workers, and coastal communities. The agreement included the interim protection of twenty intact rainforest valleys amounting to 1.5 million acres, moratoria on logging in sixty-eight other valleys totaling 2.2 million acres, and mitigation and transition funds for workers and communities. These agreements have now given way to detailed set of land-use recommendations for British Columbia's central coast whereby about one third of the area will be protected from logging and the balance subject to a new "ecosystem based management" system. While this is less than demanded by some groups, it is an historic reconciliation of conservation, communities, and industry around a plan that offers both support for a new future for communities based on sustainable use as well as protection for the critical habitat of the spirit bear.

Much still needs to be done to solidify this agreement and extend its principals to other areas in the region. Key to this is an ambitious effort to raise $120 million Canadian dollars to act as a community reinvestment fund. Half coming from government and half from private donors, the fund will be used to provide seed money and loans for new businesses in First Nations communities in order to diversify the economy away from sole dependence on extractive industries, such as logging and mining. The

future of this historic agreement will be built around achieving and maintaining community engagement and support for a greener, more sustainable economy. As has been observed by Scott Russell Sanders, "No matter
what the legal protections on the ground, no land will be safe from harm
without people committed to caring for it, year after year, generation after
generation. All conservation must therefore aim at fostering an ethic of
stewardship."[3]

Putting the strength of the market behind conservation by eliciting
customer interest in green sources of wood and sound harvesting practices is gaining acceptance, especially in the North America and Europe.
A key element is a strategy known as "certification." The concept is simple,
give customers the ability to distinguish between sustainably harvested
products and those coming from poorly managed or illegally harvested
forests and they will vote with their wallets. Most certification systems—
and there are some fifty worldwide—follow the general model established
for financial audits with standards set by an independent nonprofit board,
and auditors—qualified professional ecologists and foresters—who review and certify compliance. Companies whose lands meet the standards
can advertise and label their products. In the forest industry many such
schemes are being developed in individual countries but the largest and
longest established is the Forest Stewardship Council, offering worldwide
certification programs.

At least one state in the United States is trying to use certification efforts to attract business. Maine is the most forested state in the union, with
over 90 percent covered in trees. It's also a region that is being hard hit by
globalization; its smaller mills and old infrastructure are no match for state-
of-the-art paper and pulp plants overseas. Governor John Baldacci has
launched the Maine Forest Certification Initiative to move most of the state's
forest project industry to a greener strategy. With 6.5 million acres of land
already certified, Maine hopes to get at least 10 million acres under independent third-party certification by 2006. Already the state has moved to

certify its nearly five hundred thousand acres of publicly owned working forests under both the Sustainable Forest Initiative (SFI) and Forest Stewardship Council (FSC), certification initiatives common in the United States.

Some conservationists openly question whether certification makes a difference, pointing with suspicion to the industry's sponsored SFI program, which among other things does not mandate independent third-party inspections of a company's practices. Although most of the industry has moved to independent evaluations, some, even while touting the green practices, resist the notion of letting others monitor their harvesting. Jim Quinn, the former CEO of a forest products company in the Pacific Northwest and one of the leaders in the certification movement in the United States, thinks such resistance is misplaced. "A company would never dream of avoiding an independent audit of its financial books—their shareholders would never stand for this. Shareholders also have a right to an independent assessment of whether their forests are being well managed for the long term." Another issue that certification systems are struggling with is what to do about fiber provided to mills from outside their ownership. For example, Mead Westvaco and International Paper have been leaders in certifying their own forests but only about 30 percent of the pulp they use comes from their own lands.[4] Even the reportedly stringent FSC certification requires only 17 percent of the fiber be from certified forests to qualify for use of the FSC label. These weaknesses make many still skeptical about the real impact.

Questions persist about certification's long-term impact on the forests themselves. The scientific debate will take years to play out but there are some indications that management practices are changing for the better. I asked Tony Lyons, former director of procurement at Mead Westvaco's Maine–New Hampshire operations, about the value of certification. "Before certification, we used to pay our logging contractors a premium to deliver wood during the mud season. Our certification review told us that operating heavy equipment in the forest when it was so wet was doing a lot of damage to tree roots and compacting the soil, so we needed to change. We modified the financial incentives to encourage our wood suppliers to get the wood into the mill before spring breakup." It's a small example but over time the impact on forests may be significant.

But would the focus on making Maine the center of a greener forest products industry pay off? David Refkin, president of TI Paperco Inc., delivered the answer.[5] TI stands for Time Inc., the publisher of 135 magazines in the United States and abroad and owner of eight book companies. TI Paperco manages the paper needs of these and other Time Warner divisions. As the largest purchaser of magazine grades of paper in the world, TI's wallet is one of the biggest and most important ones to the industry. As part of Time Warner's commitment to corporate environmental performance, Refkin announced that Time would increase Maine's share of TI Paperco's business by 33 percent, resulting in Maine's providing 16 percent of all of the paper sourced by the company. This increase translates into an immediate jump of ten thousand tons of finished paper products— and more if the market improves. In committing to the purchase, Refkin observed, "Our strategy is to reward leaders and encourage laggards. I've told more than a couple of CEO's that their companies are laggards. We don't do business with people with egregious policies. Maine has shown it's a leader in moving toward a Greener Forest Products Industry."

Time's conversion to green leader was not an overnight transition. Starting in 1991, Time was the focus of a campaign led by Greenpeace, urging change in the company's paper policies. In 1992, the advocacy group, Environmental Defense Fund, asked Refkin to investigate methods for conserving paper use, thus reducing harmful impact on the environment. Time's paper consumption results in over 7 million trees being cut every year. The three years of joint effort led to a clear message: use less paper, buy from responsible producers, and recycle as much as you can.

Time has set ambitious goals for itself. North American paper suppliers already get one third of their wood from certified forests; the figure is 60 percent for Europe, where sustainable forestry is further advanced. By the end of 2006, Time expects certified forests to be the source for 80 percent of the wood used in making its paper. And in what will be good news to TNC's Indonesian program, Refkin says, "We avoid buying paper from the coast rainforest of British Columbia, which environmentalists say is critically endangered—and paper from places such as Brazil and Indonesia, where illegal logging is devastating tropical rainforests."[6]

A new report released in 2003 by IBM Business Consulting Services confirms that major customers of the logging industry are shifting their purchases toward more environmentally friendly products especially where controversy may spill over to their own company.[7] The message is clear: green customers are showing that they can help create greener companies whose new business practices are translating into effective conservation on the ground. As Martin Leighton, a crusty Maine woodsman once observed, "You know, any solution will have to do with individual solutions. We've all got to change our ways. We can't expect to keep on adding billions of people and expect the planet to keep supporting us. We each have to get our own individual houses in order. Then we can demand that these woods be taken care of properly."[8] Customers have enormous power and it is clear that by using this power, equipped with tools like certification, the practices of business can be moved toward a sustainable future that supports both the needs of communities and natural environment alike.

Box 7.1

Forest Certification Resources

Forest Stewardship Council
1155 30th Street NW, Suite 300
Washington, D.C. 20007
Phone: 202-342-0413
Fax: 202-342-6589
E-mail: info@fscus.org
Website: www.fscus.org

"The Forest Stewardship Council was created to change the dialogue about and the practice of sustainable forestry worldwide. This impressive goal has in many ways been achieved, yet there is more work to be done. FSC sets forth principles, criteria, and standards that span economic, social, and environmental concerns. The FSC standards represent the world's strongest system for guiding forest management toward sustainable outcomes. Like the forestry profession itself, the FSC system includes stakeholders with a diverse array of perspectives on a well-managed and sustainable forest. While the discussion continues, the FSC standards for forest management have now been applied in over 57 countries around the world."

Sustainable Forest Initiative
American Forest & Paper Association®
1111 Nineteenth Street, NW, Suite 800
Washington, D.C. 20036
Website:www.aboutsfi.org

"The Sustainable Forestry Initiative® (SFI) program is a comprehensive system of principles, objectives and performance measures developed by professional foresters, conservationists and scientists, among others, that combines the perpetual growing and harvesting of trees with the long-term protection of wildlife, plants, soil and water quality. There are currently over 136 million acres of forestland in North America enrolled in the SFI® program, making it among the world's largest sustainable forestry programs."

8

Tax Credits for Conservation

Fifty-four percent of Americans manage to buy $5.2 billion worth of a liquid [water] that just a generation ago was thought to be completely free, clean and rightfully ours as living beings....How might our future be different if we spend that $5.2 billion not on bottled water but on protecting water and its movements—the rivers, aquifers, lakes, oceans and wetlands that are the stuff of life?

—Peter Forbes, *The Great Remembering*

In 1999, Bridgewater Hydraulics, a small Connecticut company supplying water to the Bridgewater area, announced that it was being acquired by Kelda, a British-based services company.[1] This would not have been conservation news except that soon after the acquisition, Kelda let it quietly be known that 15,300 acres of forestland surrounding the company reservoirs in western Connecticut might be sold. Only a few years earlier, the company put 780 acres on the block near the Devil's Den preserve of The Nature Conservancy (TNC), horrifying local residents who had come to think of this land as permanently protected. Only a last minute deal costing the state $12.7 million saved the day. The sale of the Bridgewater lands would require regulatory scrutiny, but as David Sutherland, TNC's government affairs director explained, "My biggest fear was that we might find ourselves pitting the interests of urban residents looking for rate relief against suburban dwellers looking to protect open space. Everyone might lose in that debate." The price tag for a preemptive protection effort—$193 million according to appraisals—seemed out of reach, even in this affluent section of Connecticut.

The Kelda lands are the largest uninterrupted stretch of forests and streams in western Connecticut, and a hastily formed coalition began searching for options. As a group spokesperson observed, "For generations, Connecticut residents have counted on lands owned by water companies and electric utilities as a constant feature of the landscape. Now this century-old compact is threatened." The Kelda lands were only part of the lands protected by these informal utility agreements. In Connecticut, 130,000 acres are held by utilities, and the precedent of selling these lands threatened to unravel a long tradition of protecting the land.

The Kelda situation is part of a larger debate within the drinking-water industry. In 1999, the City of Milwaukee announced that the bacteria *cyclosporine* had contaminated its water and caused dozens of deaths and thousands of suspected illnesses; the news sent shock waves through water utilities. For years the industry had been dueling with the EPA over safe drinking-water standards mandating expensive clean-water treatment plants to replace a hodge-podge of reservoirs and wells supplying the nation's major urban areas. The events in Milwaukee were a tragic confirmation of EPA fears.

The creation of the Adirondack Forest Preserve in New York marked the beginning of a 150-year-old tradition of government efforts to buy forestland for water-supply protection. Gradually, water districts had become major owners of forestland throughout New England and New York. But in the face of urbanization and increased demands for safe water, it seemed inevitable that additional treatment was the way of the future, potentially rendering watershed forest protection efforts redundant. However, not all water districts see an either/or proposition—protect watersheds or build treatment plants. New York City has endorsed a combination strategy: increase protection around the Catskills—New York's most important water resource—and build smaller, less intensive treatment plants. But for many smaller water districts and local companies, the choices were few: consolidate with other, stronger companies or face escalating costs for treating water.

This larger debate was played out in the Kelda acquisition. After steadily buying up smaller water companies in the United States, Kelda now owns water companies serving fifty-three communities in Connecticut, Massachusetts, and New Hampshire. Selling 15,300 acres of forestland would give Kelda the capital to pay for its acquisitions and much needed modernization efforts. Initially the coalition appealed for Kelda to donate easements, and when that request met a deaf ear, called for the creation of a regional water authority to take over Kelda's service area. Eventually, the company recognized the seriousness of its situation and quietly signaled its interest in developing a solution with the state and conservation groups. Setting the stage for one of the largest conservation deals in U.S. history, this negotiation is an extraordinary example of how tax incentives and credits can motivate companies to choose land protection over development.

At a cost of nearly $200 million the land deal was much more than the state's Open Space Matching Grants Program could afford. In the previous year only $12 million in grants had been available for the entire state. A bigger solution was imperative. Fortunately, Connecticut had recently enacted a law offering corporations a state tax credit of 50 percent of the value of the conservation land being donated. With this ingredient in hand, the state and TNC's Connecticut chapter crafted an offer: the state would offer $90 million in order to purchase the lands in a "bargain sale," and Kelda would gift the balance to the state for the new tax credit. The value of this package came close to what Kelda would have gained after tax from an outright sale of the lands but without the politically charged fight any proposed development would have created. The state tax credit of 50 percent on a gift of $103 million would yield a whopping $51.5 million in tax benefits even though the company indicated that it would be able to only use about $12 million of the state credits and an additional $10 million in savings on its federal income tax. Still, the prospect of $22 million in credits was sufficient to bring the company to agreement. To raise the $90 million, TNC agreed to fundraise for $10 million in private donations, to be matched by a state appropriation. In the end, the package of tax incentives and cash more than made up for Kelda's potential profits from an uncertain and potentially litigious development deal that might have taken a decade or more to materialize. The land was purchased by the state in late 2001.

In reflecting on the deal, David Sutherland confirmed that the tax credits were the key ingredient in getting both the company and the Connecticut legislature to the table. "Raising the state's $80 million share was tough going and any more than that would have been impossible in the fiscal climate. The fact that millions more in credits were on the table did not seem to bother anyone because they did not require an appropriation by the legislature." The Kelda transaction demonstrates that credits can make a difference in paying for transactions and in encouraging companies to come to an agreement on price. Like in most great conservation transactions, a combination of factors—credits, money raised through more conventional means, and a political climate supportive of reaching agreement, were all essential ingredients in achieving the desired results.

Although Connecticut is the only state with credits for corporate gifts such as Kelda's, sixteen states have adopted tax credits and incentives to help private landowners do the right thing. The granddaddy of all tax programs and arguably still the most successful is North Carolina's. Enacted in 1983, that state's Conservation Tax Credit Program provides benefits to individuals and corporate taxpayers who donate conservation lands or

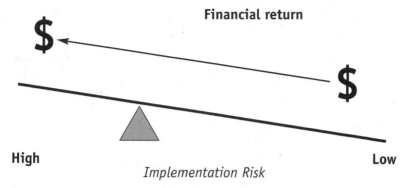

Financial return

High   **Low**

Implementation Risk

Maximize Development Option
- High risk of regulatory disapproval
- Public Outcry
- Market Risk- sale of lots
- Many years to realize

Conservation Sale with Tax Credits
- Strong Community support
- Tax Credits in Place
- Government leadership support
- Sale in near term

Figure 8.1

Kelda's Decision Calculus

easements to a state or local government agency or a qualified nonprofit. These landowners may claim a state tax credit for 25 percent of the value of the donated property. Current maximum donation levels are set at $250,000 for individuals and $500,000 for corporations; the legislature has steadily increased these levels since 1983, when individuals were limited to $5,000. Qualifying donations must provide specified public benefits, such as public beach access, public access to trails and water, protected habitat for fish and wildlife conservation, and land protection. Each donation must be certified by the state's Department of Environment and Natural Resources. As of October 1998, nearly thirty-three thousand acres of land, with a total value of $80 million, have been protected under the program. Because tax returns are confidential, it is difficult to know the actual dollar value of the tax credits claimed. According to a study by

economist Bonny Moellenbrock, published in *Popular Government*, estimated conservation donations between 1983 and 1995 were made at a
"cost" of $3.5 million to the state in lost taxes, or, looking from another
perspective, 8.5 percent of the value of the land contributed. Clearly, tax
incentives are cost-effective conservation tools.

In the late 1990s Colorado created one of the most generous conservation tax programs with an unusual twist. Landowners donating easements may sell the tax credits to individuals or corporations that can more
readily use the tax credits. This is important in a state where ranchers are
often "land rich" and income poor. As in Kelda's case, credits are only as
good as the ability to use them. This ability to sell credits has caused the
program to boom. Mike Strugar of the Conservation Resources Center in
Boulder says his group negotiated 155 transactions in 2003 worth $14 mil-
lion, up sharply from $3.3 million in 2002. Overall, sales of tax credits may
have topped $24 million statewide. One of the state's oldest land trusts,
Colorado Open Lands, tripled its easement activity in 2003 to thirteen
thousand acres under easement—one very tangible indication that credits work.[2]

A new law in New Mexico allows individuals who donate land or a
conservation easement to reduce their state income tax by up to 50
percent of the value of the gift. Here's an example: a New Mexico couple
in the 30 percent tax bracket donates an easement worth two hundred
thousand dollars. Their state credit of one hundred thousand dollars (the
maximum provided by the law) may be used over a twenty-year period.
Meanwhile, the couple gets a full federal-tax deduction for the amount
of the gift, a return of about sixty thousand dollars. Their lower adjusted
gross income also lowers their estate taxes, leaving them with a total benefit
of perhaps $170,000—nearly as much as the market value of the easement.
"That proves a serious incentive for land conservation activity," says Robert
M. Findling, director of conservation projects for TNC in New Mexico.

According to Phil Tabas, an expert on tax incentives who has followed these developments for nearly twenty-five years, states have taken three different approaches to state tax incentives:

Incentives for the gifts of conservation land or easements. These include the North Carolina and New Mexico programs, which grant tax credits for these gifts. At least seven other states have adopted their own variations.

Other states have adopted *incentives for habitat management* through their tax codes. A 1995 Arkansas law provides a landowner with a state income-tax credit of up to five thousand dollars for wetland restoration expenses. Oregon allows corporate forest landowners a state income-tax credit for up to 30 percent of the amount expended for the reforestation of underproductive forestlands. In Idaho since 1998, residents have been able to take an income-tax credit for management expenditures related to the conservation of sensitive plant and animal communities and the protection of water quality.

Finally, some states have provided *incentives to ease the burden of owning conservation lands.* Under a 1986 Maryland law, landowners can donate a conservation easement to the Maryland Environmental Trust, a state-affiliated land trust that coholds conservation easements with many local land trusts and receive 100 percent property-tax credits on unimproved conservation land (excluding house lots) during the first fifteen years after the easement is established. Since 1987, approximately forty-one thousand acres in some 340 transactions have benefited from these provisions. Many other states have "Farm and Open Space" or "Forest Use" tax legislation that grants current-use taxation status to property in these categories, to encourage the maintenance of these land uses in the face of suburban development pressure.

In the Kelda transaction, a combination of strategies was necessary to make the deal come together, but clearly the tax incentives were the critical final ingredient. The deal allowed Kelda to declare, "The transaction allows us to play an important role in the preservation of open space for all of Connecticut's citizens as we work to continuously provide an ample supply of clean, safe water to our customers."[3] A win for the company and a win for the environment.

Federal tax credits offer even more promise for conservation efforts. For businesses and individuals, saving money on federal taxes is an even more powerful motivator than saving on state taxes. Most land trusts are very familiar with charitable-gift rules and information that encourages potential donors to make gifts through easements and property of high-conservation value. Proper procedures are paramount, and the importance of adherence to appraisal and valuation rules has never been greater. Easements are undergoing scrutiny from both the media and government officials, who are concerned that manipulations of appraisals are inflating benefits to donors and giving them tax shelters worth more than the value received by conservation organizations. In 2003, The Washington Post, in a series of stinging investigative articles directed at TNC, made allegations of insider sales with trustees and other closely affiliated people, suggesting conflicts of interest in evaluating easement gifts and sales. Recently, TNC adopted new policies that prohibit transactions with trustees, board members, staff, and even corporations or partnerships in which a TNC-related party holds more than 5 percent of the ownership.

Few other land trusts have as strict a policy, but the Land Trust Alliance is currently looking at similar procedures for its members. All this vigilance points to the need for careful legal and financial work as part of any easement or fee sale with federal or state tax deductions or credits. However, it must be noted that the land trust community has completed thousands of conservation easement transactions with well-intentioned donors in transactions that are scrupulously honest: selling only when the conservation value is demonstrable and, for their charitable donation, receiving a tax benefit that is beyond reproach.

Although federal deductions for conservation deals will continue to be scrutinized, a new avenue for working with federal tax incentives is being pioneered in an innovative partnership between TNC and Coastal Enterprises, Inc. (CEI). In the waning days of the Clinton administration, a new federal program called the New Market Tax Credit (NMTC) program was established. Patterned after the highly successful federal-housing tax credits, to encourage the development of low-income housing, the program offers tax credits for equity investors in low-income areas of the country. Back in 2001 when regulations for the program were being developed, I noticed that many of the low-income areas of the country overlapped with forested areas of conservation interest. This should be no surprise, given the hard times many rural economies have faced in the last decade as high-paying sawmill and paper manufacturing jobs declined in the face of foreign competition. Working with Ron Phillips, CEI's creative president, we came up with the concept of using these tax credits to attract investors to working forestlands, where the long-term goal was sustainable forestry and not liquidation and development. The concept was simple: offer tax credits linked to low-cost capital in exchange for a conservation easement on the property, thus insuring long-term sustainable forest management.

In April 2003, the Department of Treasury awarded the first $2.5 billion in tax credits to financial intermediaries; CEI-TNC's efforts were rewarded with an allocation of $65 million in credits to the consortium, to be used to reward investors committed to the sustainable management of their land. Qualifying investments earn a the tax credit of 39 percent, spread over seven years at the rate of 5 percent per year for the first three years and 6 percent per year for the ensuing four years. In a second round of awards the Treasury increased the amount of credits devoted to this effort by an additional $64 million.

In one example of how these credits can be used for conservation, the CEI-TNC partnership used a portion of these credits to enhance TNC's low-interest note to Great Northern Paper. As discussed in chapter 3, TNC had made a low-interest, $36 million loan to the company in exchange for a conservation easement on two hundred thousand acres of high-value conservation land adjacent to Baxter State Park. To fund the loan TNC had used short-term funding from its revolving land-protection fund, which it urgently needed to repay.

The hunt for a financial partner to buy out the Katahdin loan with tax credits to enhance its return to more market based levels commenced in earnest during the summer of 2003. At first financial institutions were lukewarm to NMTCs because of the uncertainties in a new program. Fortunately, Allan Wieman, an investment manager at GE Capital, the behemoth of structured financing, immediately saw the opportunity to use the credits to jumpstart GE's efforts to grow its forestland-lending business. The partnership of GE with TNC-CEI ultimately resulted in TNC's loan being repaid in February 2004 with a new tax-credit-enhanced loan from GE.

Now that the NMTC program is up and running with its first investment behind it, the concept of loans tied to conservation outcomes and facilitated by tax credits is in full swing. The partnership has already closed three additional NMTC loans linked to forestland and is contemplating others. It is also considering new categories of investments. For instance, low-interest loans, made possible with tax credits, may help finance a manufacturing company in Arizona that will source its wood from small-diameter trees in the national forests, all part of a plan to end catastrophic wild fires. Ecologists believe that the removal of years of accumulated wood debris, a legacy of decades of misguided fire-suppression efforts, will allow managers to reintroduce the natural, low-intensity fires necessary to keep Arizona's forests healthy.

Over the last decade, state and federal tax credits and incentives have proven to be a creative and effective way to get conservation accomplished. When tax credits favor landowners, they are sometimes more motivated to consider a conservation outcome for their land. Often these deals provide at least as much cash in sellers' pockets as simple land sales, but at a much lower cost to the land trust or state agency. As we search for new sources of funds to meet the needs for protection of critical properties, deploying these incentives needs to be part our tool kit.

Box 8.1

Ways to Utilize New Market Tax Credits for Conservation

Link to land conservation purchases

Low-interest financing to companies in exchange for easements or fee
    interests—must be linked to jobs and sustainable development, not bio-
    diversity
Low-interest loans to conservation groups (for example, a working forest
    with timber revenue acquired by TNC and partially financed with credits)

Work with business activities that support a conservation mission

Business to utilize small diameter wood (for example, projects in Arizona)
Investment in ecotourism activities linked to lands purchase (for example,
    AMC's purchase of Katahdin Iron Works property to create a new back-
    country recreation system in Maine)

Box 8.2

Tax Credit and Incentives

Tax Credits

Conservation opportunities are growing for land trusts in states offering
tax benefits. But many landowners are simply not aware of them, and
many states have not devised a method for applying them at the scale
of Connecticut's Kelda transaction.

Creating or adding to legislation is a key policy opportunity in many states.
While much of the focus on tax incentives has been on the federal
level, increasing state income-tax levels create reasons to consider new
local legislation.

Finally, Congress has considered but not yet enacted legislation to change
the tax-code advantages of selling or gifting conservation land or easements. Tax credits against the income or gain from the sale of land
for conservation purposes could encourage land-rich but income-poor
owners of high-value forest and ranch lands to release their property.

Easements and Donations of Land

The Land Trust Alliance is an excellent resource on easements and maintains a code of practices for land trusts on valuing easements and structuring transactions.

Land Trust Alliance
1331 H Street NW, Suite 400
Washington, D.C. 20005-4734
Phone: 202-638-4725
Website: www.lta.org

New Market Tax Credits

This federal program offers 39 percent tax credits on eligible equity investments in low-income areas thorough out the country. The credits are

continued

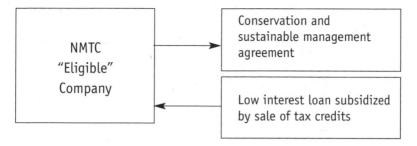

Figure 8.2

Using New Market Tax Credits for Conservation.

Box 8.2 continued

guarded through financial intermediaries selected by the Department of Treasury in a comparative process. With $15 billion authorized, it's a major program and if even a small percentage of the funding efforts can be linked to conservation and sustainable development projects, the impact could be significant.

For Information on the Federal Program visit www.cdfifund.gov. This site also has interactive maps that let you look at any geographic location in United States to determine its eligibility for credits.

For information about the NMTC partnership between Coastal Enterprises, Inc. and TNC, contact Steve Weems, senior vice president, Coastal Enterprises, Inc.

Coastal Enterprises, Inc.
36 Water Street
P.O. Box 268
Wiscasset, ME 04578
E-mail: Steveweems@ceimaine.org
Phone: 207-882-7552.

Table 8.1

Summary of State and Federal Income Tax Credits for Conservation, April 2003

Agency	Title and summary	Easement/land type	Type of donee	Amount of credit	Individual limit	Carry over
U.S.–IRS	Charitable donations	Any gift of an interest in land	Government agency or nonprofit	100% of the value of the donation as a deduction	Generally no more than 30% per year of taxable income for individuals and 10% for corporations	5 years
U.S.–Department of Treasury	New Market Tax Credit Program	For equity investments in businesses located in qualifying census districts. See www.cdfifund.gov	Through intermediaries designated by U.S.	39% overall, 5% for first 3 years and 6% for the last 4 years	None	7 years
California	Natural Heritage Preservation Tax Credit Act	Five designated types of land, eligibility determined by Board.	55% fair market value (FMV)	Includes bargain sales	No	7 years
Colorado	Credit against tax-conservation easements	Easements only	Government agency or designated nonprofit	100% FMV of 1st $100k, 40% of next $400k	$100,000 + $160,000 = $260,000, up to $20k as a refund	20 years

Table 8.1 (continued)

Agency	Title and summary	Easement/land type	Type of donee	Amount of credit	Individual limit	Carry over
Connecticut	An Act concerning Various Tax Reductions, Exemptions and Credits	Any land or interest in land, including bargain sales Corporate donations only	Government agency or nonprofit	50%	No	10 years
Delaware	Land and Historic Resources Tax Credit	Any land or interest in land conveyed for the purpose of open space, natural resource or biodiversity conservation or historic preservation	Government agency or nonprofit	40% FMV	$50,000	5 years
Maryland	Tax Credit for Donations of Conservation Easements	Any land that will serve the public interest—woodlands, wetlands, farmland, historic areas, wild and scenic rivers, undisturbed natural areas	Designated nonprofits	100% of appraised value of easement	$5,000/yr. up to $80,000	15 years

Table 8.1 (continued)

Agency	Title and summary	Easement/land type	Type of donee	Amount of credit	Individual limit	Carry over
Mississippi	An Income Tax Credit for Donations of Land for Priority Conservation Sites and Riparian Corridor Areas	Lands to protect stream bank habitats and stability and to protect high biodiversity sites with exemplary natural communities or species of special concern or T/E species	Government agency or qualified nonprofit	50% of "Allowable Transaction Costs" (e.g., appraisal, baseline report, legal documents and title costs)	$10,000	10 years
New Mexico	New Mexico Land Conservation Incentives Act	Any land or interest in land conveyed for the purpose of open space, natural resource or biodiversity conservation, outdoor recreation, farmland and forestland pres., historic pres., and land conservation purposes	Government agency or qualified non-profit	50% FMV	$100,000	20 years
North Carolina	Credit for certain real property donations	Any property useful for public beach access, access to waters or trails, fish and wildlife conservation, or other similar land conservation purposes	Government agency or nonprofit	25% FMV	Originally $5,000 1989-amended to $250,000 for Ind., $500,000 for Corps	5 years

Table 8.1 (continued)

Agency	Title and summary	Easement/land type	Type of donee	Amount of credit	Individual limit	Carry over
South Carolina	South Carolina Conservation Incentives Act	Land claimed and qualified for a federal deduction for a gift of land for conservation, as defined by Sec. 170 (h)	Qualified conservation organization	25% FMV	$250 per acre, with a maximum credit of $52,500 per year	Carry-over allowed until all the value of credit is claimed
Virginia	Virginia Land Conservation Incentives Act of 1999	Land or interest in land conveyed for purpose of agricultural or forest use, open space, conservation or historic preservation	Government agency or r.onprofit	50% FMV	$50K for 2000, $75K for 2001, $100K for 2002 and thereafter	5 years

This table was prepared by Phil Tabas, general counsel to The Nature Conservancy and is used by permission of the Nature Conservancy.

9

Incentives for Working Landscapes

Typically, property owners are not compensated for the services that natural assets on their land provide to society: With rare exception, the owners of coastal wetlands are not paid for the abundance of seafood the wetlands nurture, nor are owners of tropical forest compensated for that ecosystem's contribution to the pharmaceutical industry and climate stability. As a result, many crucial types of ecosystem capital are undergoing rapid degradation and depletion. Compounding the problem is that the importance of ecosystem services is often widely appreciated only upon their loss.

—Gretchen Daily and Katherine Ellison, *The New Economy of Nature*

Piping plovers and least terns have an unfortunate habit of picking the most expensive real estate in the United States for their nesting habitats. The interface between sand dunes and the ocean is coveted by many other species during the nesting season, including summer tourists. What's more, the bird species, especially in the northern fringes of their nesting range, have a bad habit of switching from beach to beach every few years, surprising wildlife managers and confounding efforts to purchase nesting habitats. With a single acre of prime beachfront going for as much as five hundred thousand dollars even in rural states like Maine, acquiring the "wrong" place is a career-challenging event for government and nonprofit executives alike.

Dealing with the fickle habitat requirements of many species has increased the recognition that, with modest consideration for their needs, many endangered species can do just fine on privately owned working lands. In fact, many species need active management to survive, and in more than a few cases, a cooperative landowner can make the difference, eliminating the need for intrusive government regulations or conservation ownership. A case in point is the black-capped vireo, a threatened migratory bird found in the open brushy lands typical of the hill country of central Texas. Without periodic fires or clearing of overstory trees, vireo habitat is lost rapidly. A heavy-handed regulatory approach does little to encourage landowners to actively manage for the bird; in fact, these regulations can have the perverse effect of reducing the viability of the bird's habitat as overstory plants proliferate, unchecked by ranchers. Strict penalties for disturbing vireos have understandably caused landowners to shy away from any management whatsoever. They simply ignore the areas, choosing a pattern of "compliance" that will eventually result in disaster for the vireo. As one group has noted, "Unfortunately the highest level of assurance that a property owner will not face an endangered species issue is to maintain the property in a condition such that protected species can not occupy the property."[1] Landowners will need incentives rather than intrusive regulations if some species are to survive.

The impact of *perverse incentives* that prevent landowners from conducting much needed management on ecologically sensitive areas has been a special focus of the Environmental Defense Fund. One of their landmark studies concluded: "Most listed species will continue to decline unless landowners actively manage the habitat for their benefit. In fact, researchers have found that recovery plans for some 305 species—an estimated 63 percent—depend on 'some form of management.'"[2]

Controversy, however, plagues the federal government's effort to moderate its historic "disincentives," created through regulatory prohibitions. Some environmental advocates, citing the regulatory intent of the Clean

Air, Water, and Endangered Species Acts, believe landowners are required to take action and not simply be financially "encouraged to do it." As Bill Weeks, a lawyer and the former COO of The Nature Conservancy (TNC), thoughtfully observes in *Beyond the Ark,* "Protected areas—the natural stronghold of the net [ecosystems]—could perhaps amount to 15 percent of the landscape if we make heroic efforts to make that happen. The fate of the net will, however, be determined by what happens to the remaining 85 percent of the landscape."[3] Weeks makes it is clear that creating innovative partnerships and incentives for owners of working lands is not a simple option; it's a requirement for achieving conservation success.

The Landowner Incentive Program (LIP) of the Department of the Interior's Fish and Wildlife Service is among the tools for effecting change. This program provides financial incentives for private landowners willing to protect at-risk species on their property. In announcing $26 million in LIP grants in 2004, Secretary Gail Norton declared, "LIP is based on the idea of working with private landowners to enhance habitat with threatened or endangered species on the property." With LIP funds in hand, U.S. Fish and Wildlife plans to provide technical and financial assistance to landowners to conserve and manage endangered species, including piping plovers and least terns.

Maine's LIP grant program is a good example of how small investments can pay off in conservation results. Consecutive years of predation by mink have reduced Stratton Island's arctic, common and roseate terns, from over 2000 pairs in 2001 to fewer than 350 today.[4] According to the Maine Audubon Society, the island's owner, controlling these predators is essential to the survival of the birds. Without active management, conservation ownership will not ensure the survival of the system. "Letting nature take its course" will result in significant losses. With LIP funds, Audubon is now carefully controlling the populations of predators in order to ensure the survival of the terns.

Small investments in management can also be a good prevention strategy. In Colorado, the Division of Wildlife has been using LIP funds to restore Front Range habitat for the Preble's Meadow jumping mouse, a federally listed species, and for the Gunnison sage grouse, which is a potential endangered species. Jim Guthrie, administrator of the program, cites the long-ranging debate about whether a state should focus efforts on species already endangered or those that are potentially endangered. "The policy of our state is to work on both."[5]

In an effort to encourage landowners to protect threatened species, the Endangered Species Act has added Safe Harbor or "no surprise" agreements with landowners. Beginning in 1982, Congress amended the law to allow private landowners to apply for a permit that would allow the incidental loss of an individual endangered plant or animal in exchange for a broader habitat conservation plan. The effect is twofold: to minimize the potential impact of management on the species and to encourage management actions that will maintain and expand the population. More than two hundred such plans have been created at significant expense to landowners, because they offer them certainty. Harsh regulatory proceedings or fines will not be applied in cases of loss of an individual in an endangered population or, conversely, of an individual in an expanding population that is thriving on good management activities by the landowner. As EDF has pointed out, "The incentive for these companies is that they will have a steady timber supply for their mills for the length of the permit. Since companies have often invested heavily in these mills, such certainty is immensely valuable"[6]

Nowhere has the experiment with incentives been more extensive than in the federal government's agricultural funding programs known as the Farm Bill. The Environmental Quality Incentives Program (EQIP), created in the 1996 Farm Bill, offers farmers financial, educational, and technical assistance for conservation practices. The funding for these programs has increased steadily from an initial $275 million to $1.3 billion in FY 2007. EQIP can fund a broad range of conservation practices and projects: funding storage systems to better contain manure, fencing animals out of streams, and developing alternative watering sources are among the initiatives to protect water and air quality. Other practices frequently funded include conservation tillage, pest management, grassed waterways, wetland habitat restoration, brush management, proscribed burning, forest-stand improvement, and stream habitat improvement. EDF has tracked success stories from EQIP programs across the country benefiting from funding.

Box 9.1

Environmental Quality Incentives Program (EQIP) Projects

Saving the Pallid Sturgeon

The U.S. Fish and Wildlife Service and the U.S. Army Corps of Engineers planned periodic releases of large quantities of water from the Fort Peck Reservoir to help save the sturgeon. The rising water levels—which are intended to mimic historic natural Missouri River flooding—will occur each spring for three years, increasing to a higher level each year. The goal of the "spring rise" is to trigger the pallid sturgeon's spawning mechanism.

Over one hundred farms downstream from the spring rise will be flooded, threatening the livelihood of those farmers. The Montana NRCS launched a special EQIP initiative to help farmers retrofit and relocate their irrigation systems, reduce or eliminate the potential for negative water quality impacts (mostly from fuel tanks), and create wildlife habitat along the Missouri River. The state NRCS directed $328,000 of its 2003 EQIP funds to eleven farmers and set aside an additional $300,000 in 2004 and 2005 to aid affected growers. Through the use of ranking criteria, the Montana

NRCS created a priority list to assure that farmers with the most urgent needs would be the first to receive help at each flood stage level over the project's three-year course. Pump sites at the susceptible lower elevations on the riverbank received the highest points, ensuring a quicker response during the landowner-application ranking process.

Improving Grizzly and Trout Habitat

NRCS in Conrad, Montana has partnered with landowners Robert and Ali Newkirk and state and federal wildlife agencies to restore habitat for threatened grizzly bears (*Ursus arctos*) and wild trout along a three-quarter mile reach of Dupuyer Creek. The area, severely damaged during a 1964 flood, was cleared of riparian vegetation for farming. Subsequent uncontrolled grazing further contributed to serious streambank erosion. EQIP along with the U.S. Fish and Wildlife Service's Partners for Fish and Wildlife Program and Montana's Fish, Wildlife and Parks Future Fisheries Program funded in-stream trout habitat and streambank cover restoration and riparian area fencing. Some of the specific conservation practices implemented include bank shaping, tree revetment, root wad installation, and willow transplanting. The project created a secure travel corridor for area grizzly bears, lessening the potential for conflict with people. Reduced sedimentation and streambank erosion is improving water quality for wild rainbow trout (*Oncorhynchus mykiss*) and other species.

> From Dave White, NRCS State Conservationist in Montana as reported to Suzy Friedman, scientist and agricultural policy analyst, Environmental Defense Fund, available at www.environmentaldefense.org/article.cfm?contentid=3514.

Table 9.1

Outlays for Mandatory Agricultural Incentive Programs (Millions of dollars by fiscal year)

Program	2002 (actual)	2003 (actual)	2004 (est.)	2005 (est.)	2006 (est.)	2007 (est.)
Environmental Quality Incentives Program	$224	$504	$774	$1,016	$1,150	$1,248
Wildlife Habitat Incentive Program	$7	$22	$34	$53	$73	$82
Farmland Protection Program	$8	$54	$112	$115	$116	$103
Conservation Security program	—	—	$41	$282	$649	$846
Other mandatory programs	$2,047	$2,167	$2,217	$2,318	$2,432	$2,386
Total Mandatory Conservation Outlays	$2,286	$2,747	$3,178	$3,784	$4,420	$4,665

Other mandatory programs include Conservation Reserve Program, Wetlands Reserve Program, Grasslands Reserve program, Small Watershed Rehabilitation Program, Ground and Surface Water Conservation Program, and Agricultural Management Assistance program.

Zinn, Jeffrey. "Funding Trends": 4–10.

In sharp contrast to declining funding for traditional land conservation through the Land and Water Conservation Fund, these new Department of Agriculture programs administered through the Natural Resources Conservation Service and the Department of Agriculture are growing dramatically. The federal government has shifted its approach from sole dependence on traditional agricultural subsidies toward incentive based funding aimed at altering landowner behaviors and improving the condition of natural resources. Funding for many of these programs has been made mandatory thereby removing them from the annual appropriation process. This is achieved largely through the

---

Box 9.2

Center for Conservation Incentives, Environmental Defense Fund

The Center for Conservation Incentives, an initiative of the Environmental Defense Fund, was launched in March 2003, with major support from the Doris Duke Charitable Foundation. The Center's overarching objective is to conserve biodiversity on private lands by improving and expanding existing incentive programs and by creating new ones.

The Center (1) designs and implements model projects that demonstrate how incentive-based strategies can benefit biodiversity and foster private lands stewardship; (2) improves federal and state conservation incentive policies to make them more effective both in protecting ecosystems and in rewarding landowners who do so; (3) undertakes research and analyses to help shape both conservation incentive policies and the allocation of incentive funds; and (4) builds broad public awareness and support for private land conservation and incentive programs.

Environmental Defense Fund
257 Park Avenue South
New York, NY 10010
Phone: 212-505-2100
Fax: 212-505-2375
Website: www.environmentaldefense.org

Commodity Credit Corporation, a financing institution in the Department of Agriculture authorized to borrow up to $30 billion from the U.S. Treasury with net losses restored through the appropriation process.

Incentive programs are an opportunity for conservationists to develop new strategies to achieve results and obtain funding from unusual sources. By understanding the motives of ranchers, farmers, and foresters, conservationists can encourage best practices and proactive strategies through financial or Safe Harbor type incentives. Desirable outcomes can be achieved without using a "big stick" regulatory approach. As we move to the landscape scale in conservation strategy, landowner involvement will become the norm and not the exception. At the center of these programs is the recognition that what happens in the "other 85 percent" of the earth that will not likely be in reserves is critical to communities and the natural resource systems that sustain them. Seen in one way these programs are a shift away from traditional land protection but in the long view, engaging the powerful agricultural, ranching, and forest industries in sustainable use though incentives may well be a transformative way forward to a new economy where the needs of nature are at the center and not the edges of our system.

Box 9.3

Federal Government Programs

The Conservation Reserve Program (CRP)

The Conservation Reserve Program (CRP), is a program from the USDA Farm Service Agency (FSA) that provides financial aid including rental payments and cost-sharing for farmers, who in return plant crops such as trees and grasses that improve soil and water quality and wildlife habitat. These crops help protect millions of acres of American topsoil from erosion, increase wildlife habitat, and protect ground and surface water by reducing water runoff and sedimentation. Increasing prairie chicken populations in Colorado have been directly linked to the habitat provided by the CRP easements.

Eligibility
In order to be eligible for enrollment, croplands must have been planted with agricultural commodities during four of the six most recent years and

be capable of being planted in a normal manner with an agricultural commodity. The owner or operator must also have had control of the land for the previous twelve months. Typical enrollment with the program is for ten to fifteen years.

Funding

Funding for this program comes from the Federal Government under the Farm Bill. The funding is appropriated based on conserving a certain number of acres of land. The monetary value of the land is determined by the Commodity Credit Corporation using a variety of local indicators.

How to Apply

Enrollment in the CRP program occurs during general sign up periods only—unless the land meets certain qualifications for the FSA's continuous enrollment, which include land devoted to certain conservation practices. For more information contact your local FSA office and check out the Conservation Reserve Program website at www.fsa.usda.gov/dafp/cepd/crp.htm.

Conservation Reserve Enhancement Program (CREP)

The Conservation Reserve Enhancement Program (CREP) is an offshoot of the Conservation Reserve Program (CRP). It is targeted to conservation priority items including impacted water supplies, loss of critical habitat for threatened and endangered wildlife species, soil erosion, and reduced habitat for fish populations such as salmon. Like CRP, farmers can receive monthly financial support in the form of rent and cost-share assistance, however these and other financial incentives require the retirement of certain targeted agricultural lands. These lands are earmarked by local, state, tribal, or nongovernmental organizations who identify agricultural conservation priority areas.

continued

Box 9.3 **continued**

Eligibility

This is a limited program and is targeted toward specific states and other priority areas. Contact your local FSA office, or your county Department of Agriculture Service Center for more information or to find out if your land qualifies.

Funding

The FSA uses funding from the Conservation Reserve Program along with funding from local, state, and private resources to provide the funding for the Conservation Reserve Enhancement Program.

How to Apply

Because this program is administered by local, state, nongovernment, and tribal groups, and the land is targeted geographically, there is no application process. Participation in the program is dependent on if your area qualifies geographically and if you meet certain eligibility requirements. Contact your local FSA office or your County Department of Agriculture Service Center or visit the CREP website at www.fsa.usda.gov/dafp/cepd/crep.htm.

The Conservation Security Program (CSP)

The Conservation Security Program aids owners and operators of tribal and working land (including cropland, grassland, prairie land, improved pasture, range land, and forested land) in maintaining and increasing their conservation practices on their land. The program provides targeted financial assistance in three different tiers depending on the conservation priority determined in the application process.

Eligibility

The land must be privately owned or tribal lands, and it must fall mostly within one watershed. For each tier of funding there are more strict eligibility requirements. Take a self-assessment online, or get a self-assessment book from your local National Resource Conservation Services office.

Funding

The program is slated to get $3.77 billion over ten years, with $369 million allocated to years covered by the current Farm Bill.

How to Apply

Complete a self-assessment of the agricultural land to see if you qualify. These are available online at www.nrcs.usda.gov/programs/csp, as well as at local National Resource Conservation Service offices nationwide. After the submission of an application, it is reviewed to see if it fits into one of the several tiers of funding offered by the program. For more information contact your local USDA Service Center, listed in the telephone book under U.S. Department of Agriculture or look online at www.nrcs.usda.gov/programs/farmbill/2002/.

Environmental Quality Incentives Program (EQIP)

Originally created in the 1996 Farm Bill, and reauthorized in the 2002 Farm Bill, the Environmental Quality Incentives Program (EQIP) helps farmers and ranchers improve infrastructure and land-management practices. These funds address local issues determined on a state-by-state basis. The program offers incentives to adopt management practices in response to nutrients, manure, water irrigation, and wildlife habitat, as well as integrated pest management practices. Cost sharing covers up to 75 percent and the contract lengths are from one to ten years.

Eligibility

If you are engaged in crop or livestock production on eligible land and are interested in participating in one of the conservation initiatives in your state then you are eligible.

Funding

The program is funded through the 2002 Farm Bill.

continued

Box 9.3   continued

How to Apply

Applications are available online at
www.nrcs.usda.gov/programs/eqip/, or you can contact your local
National Resource Counsel Services office in the Department of
Agriculture.

Conservation Innovation Grants (CIG)
A subprogram of EQIP, Conservation Innovation grants (CIGs) promote environmental enhancement and protection through innovative solutions in
conjunction with agricultural production.

Eligibility
Non–Federal Government and nongovernmental organizations, tribes, as
well as individuals, may receive CI grants.

Funding
Funding comes from EQIP funds and is designated specifically for these
grants. Grant funds may cover up to 50 percent of the costs of a project,
and the recipient must come up with the remaining 50 percent matching
funds from nonfederal sources.

How to Apply

When grant money becomes available each year a notice will be
posted on the federal grants website at www.grants.gov. A notice will
also be made available at www.nrcs.usda.gov/programs/cig.

**Farm and Ranch Lands Protection Program
(Farmland Protection Program [FPP])**
The FPP provides funds to purchase easements on farmland to prevent development and to keep farmland in agricultural production. The USDA provides up to 50 percent of the fair market value of land.

Eligibility

The land must be part of a pending offer from a state, tribe, or local farm-land protection program; be privately owned; have a conservation plan; be large enough to sustain agricultural production; be accessible to markets for what the land produces; have adequate infrastructure and agricultural support services; and have surrounding parcels of land that can support long-term agricultural production. More information on eligibility is located at www.info.usda.gov/nrcs/fpcp/fpp.htm.

Funding

Funding comes from Commodity Credit Corporation under the authorization of the 1996 Farm Bill.

How to Apply

Applications for funding come from the National Resource Council Serv-ices state offices in your area. See the NRCS website for more information, www.info.usda.gov/nrcs/fpcp/fpp.htm.

Grasslands Reserve Program (GRP)

The Grasslands Reserve Program aids landowners in protecting and restor-ing their grassland, rangeland, pastureland, and shrubland while at the same time maintaining it for grazing purposes. The minimum amount of land to qualify for the program is forty acres, and there are several ease-ment and payment options.

Eligibility

Privately owned lands and tribal lands, land that contains forbs, land of ecological value for habitat rehabilitation, and land that historically con-tained forbs or grasslands are eligible for the GRP.

Funding

Funding for the GRP comes from the Commodity Credit Corporation, in as-sociation with the NRCS and FSA.

continued

Box 9.3   continued

How to Apply
Applications are available online at the NRCS website www.nrcs.usda.gov/
programs/farmbill/2002/ and www.fsa.usda.gov/dafp/GRP/default1.htm or
you can contact your local USDA Service Center, listed in the telephone
book under U.S. Department of Agriculture.

Wetlands Reserve Program (WRP)

The Wetlands Reserve Program (WRP) helps private landowners, such as
farmers and ranchers who wish to restore and protect wetlands. WRP offers
farmers and ranchers up to 100 percent reimbursement for restoring previously drained wetlands as well as financial incentives for retiring marginal
agricultural lands. There are several easement options available and the
landowner controls access to the land, however they are voluntarily re-
stricting future use.

Eligibility

Wetlands farmed under natural conditions
Farmed wetlands
Prior converted cropland
Farmed wetland pasture
Farmland that has become a wetland as a result of flooding
Rangeland, pasture, or production forestland where the hydrology has been
     significantly degraded and can be restored
Riparian areas that link protected wetlands
Lands adjacent to protected wetlands that contribute significantly to wet-
     land functions and values
Previously restored wetlands that need long-term protection

Funding
Funding for the WRP comes from the Commodity Credit Corporation, in association with the NRCS and FSA.

How to Apply

Applications are accepted through a continuous sign-up process. Applications may be obtained and filed at any time with your local USDA Service Center or conservation district office. Applications also may be obtained through USDA's e-gov Internet site at www.sc.egov.usda.gov. Enter "Natural Resources Conservation Service" in the Agency field, "Wetlands Reserve Program" in the Program Name field, and "AD-1153" in the Form Number field. For more information visit the NRCS website at www.nrcs.usda.gov/programs/wrp/.

Wildlife Habitat Incentives Program (WHIP)

The Wildlife Habitat Incentives Program (WHIP) provides technical and financial assistance to private and tribal landowners who develop their land to protect and preserve wildlife habitats. If approved, the NRCS works with the landowner to develop a management plan of the land. These landowners voluntarily limit the use of their land but retain ownership.

Eligibility

Privately owned land
Federal land when the primary benefit is on private or tribal land
State and local government land on a limited basis
Tribal land

If land is determined eligible, NRCS places emphasis on enrolling:
Habitat areas for wildlife species experiencing declining or significantly reduced populations
Practices beneficial to fish and wildlife that may not otherwise be funded
Wildlife and fishery habitats identified by local and state partners and Indian tribes in each state

Funding

Funding for WHIP comes from the Commodity Credit Corporation, in association with the NRCS.

continued

Box 9.3   continued

How to Apply

Applications are accepted through a continuous sign-up process. Applications may be obtained and filed at any time with your local USDA Service Center or conservation district office. Applications also may be obtained through USDA's e-gov Internet site at www.sc.egov.usda.gov. Click on Register to open a USDA account and then have access to a WHIP application (CCC-1200) or other USDA programs. Applications also may be accepted by cooperating conservation partners approved or designated by NRCS. For more information visit the NRCS website www.nrcs.usda.gov/programs /whip/.

Landowner Incentives Program (LIP)

The Landowner Incentives Program helps to establish or supplement existing landowner incentive programs that provide technical or financial assistance, including habitat protection and restoration to private landowners and tribal land holders.

Eligibility

Application is limited to states, federally recognized Indian tribal governments, Puerto Rico, the U.S. Virgin Islands, the Northern Mariana Islands, Guam, and American Samoa agencies with lead management responsibility for fish and wildlife resources. While local landowners are not eligible to directly receive funds, they benefit directly from the state agencies implementing the grants.

Funding

U.S. Fish and Wildlife Service administers the Landowner Incentives Program (LIP). In 2004 funding was set at $27 million, mostly provided through state Fish and Wildlife conservation agencies. Unlike the farm bill programs, the lands eligible for funding do not have to be working farmlands.

How to Apply

Instructions for applying for federal funding is available at the website www.nctc.fws.gov/fedaid/fatrain. More information is available from the Catalog of Federal Domestic Assistance at www.cdfa.gov. Click on "Search for Assistance Programs" then on "Search by Program Number" and enter number 15.633.

> The Environmental Defense Fund Conservation Incentives Program is an excellent technical resource for these programs. For more information, visit their web site at www.environmentaldefense.org/farmbill/home.cfm or at www. privatelandstewardship.org.

Part IV
The Path Forward

10

If You Build It, Will They Come?

If we are serious about conservation . . . we are going to have to come up
with competent, practical, at-home answers to the humblest human questions:
how should we live? How should we keep house? How should we provide ourselves with food, clothing, shelter, heat, light, learning, amusement, rest?
How, in short, ought we to use the world?

—Wendell Berry, *Another Turn of the Crank*

Most of this book has talked about success but in truth, not all of our efforts have achieved what we have set out to accomplish. Back in 1997, Bill
Weeks, then director of The Nature Conservancy's Center for Compatible
Economic Development, laid out a comprehensive new vision for how
conservationists could engage the engine of commerce in the protection
of the environment. A cornerstone of the new paradigm, outlined in his
book *Beyond the Ark*, was the Virginia Eastern Shore Sustainable Development Corporation (VESC), a for-profit corporation in which TNC
held a substantial interest; its purpose: "to develop and support products,
business ventures, and land uses that enhance the local economy, achieve
community goals and preserve the natural resources on the Virginia Eastern Shore." VESC proposed to launch dozens of ventures designed to create links between the local economy and land conservation. The ventures
included real estate development and tourism, clam and oyster farming,

arts and crafts, and Hayman Potato Chips. Investors included the Ford Foundation, which contributed $1 million of the initial $2.25 million in capital.

VESC's plan was to focus on three broad business efforts:[1]

Eastern Shore Products: To develop, license, and market an array of products that capture the local area's strengths and comparative advantages

Eastern Shore Venture Fund: To provide loans and investment capital to new and existing economically sound and ecologically compatible local businesses

Eastern Shore Lands: To purchase, sell, and lease sustainable agricultural lands, affordable housing, and commercial enterprises for local farmers, watermen, businesses, and citizens

As one reviewer of the project commented, "VESC was a radical approach for TNC. It was born of a recognition that its land-acquisition model was not going to be enough to protect its major land and conservation interests on the eastern shore, and from the expectation that TNC should act to improve the economy and safeguard the lifestyle of the local community."[2] TNC correctly assessed the need for new tools and new strategies for abating the pressures facing the area but ran into trouble in implementing those new approaches.

Earlier on Weeks acknowledged the challenge inherent in such an effort, observing, "Conservationists who conceive of, create and capitalize for-profit business as a conservation tool have strayed a long way from the terra firma of parks and preserves. . . .The waters in which the project is now sailing are uncharted but the course it is following is far from capricious."[3]

Despite the lofty ambitions and promise of the concepts, by mid-1999 the company collapsed in a sea of red ink. The program had underestimated the challenge of ensuring VESC would be as highly skilled as

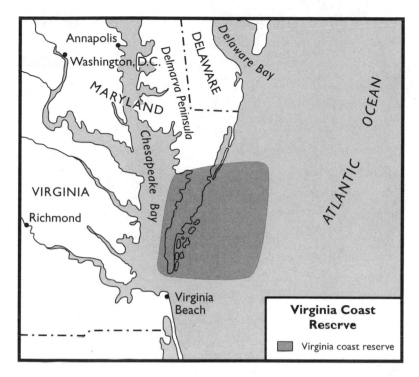

Figure 10.1
Virginia's Eastern Shore

entrepreneurs as they were as *conservationists*. The story of the VESC melt-down should be sobering to anyone thinking about compatible development efforts as part of a conservation strategy. In its analysis of the situation, the Center for Enterprise Development (CFED) laid it out in simple terms: "Flawed Concept, Flawed Business Plan, Flawed Execution." The concept for VESC had placed TNC at the center of many of the ventures—instead of a motivated entrepreneur. As the analysts pointed out, "TNC had been ill-advised to become involved in the direct operation of the business, instead of being the broker of relations, the promoter of deals, or perhaps the provider of new markets." Investing in a business is one thing, but actually starting and developing a mission-related business is a far more complex and specialized task.

One of the daunting difficulties of the eastern shore was its depressed rural economy. The business plan required VESC to launch multiple businesses at the same time, and they were widely different businesses: agricultural products, real estate development, and agriculture—all requiring significantly different expertise. In short, a venture that would have been extraordinarily challenging for teams of entrepreneurs proved impossible for VESC's modest funds and staff. Again the CFBE outlined the flaws— "from too many start-ups and inadequate market analysis to groundless and extreme optimism, unsupported assumptions, and too many roles for a hands-on CEO."

One economic success funded by the effort was a clam aquaculture industry. Designed to abate the threat of waterfront development and its related infrastructure, the final result demonstrated that the goal of conservation and those of business can diverge. According to an internal TNC evaluation of the program, "It now appears that clam aquaculture could have unintended negative consequences as the scale of operations begins to exceed sustainable levels. . . .Once unleashed, TNC can do little to control markets. Beware the law of unintended consequences—compatible economic development may create as many problems as it solves."[4] Economic systems and markets are messy, and they don't follow conservation rules.

With such a staggering broad concept and an ambitious business plan, it is no surprise that implementation fell far short of expectations. VESC's losses for the first two years of operation were over $1 million—86 percent of the company's initial capital. And the company expenses continued to increase. By 1998 the company had accumulated a deficit of nearly $2 million; without capital, the venture was dissolved in August of 1999. As Bill Weeks observed, "The business might have done better with more duct tape and less gold plated plumbing," confirming what more than one business analyst has observed: too much money leads to lack of discipline in cost control and assessment of strategies.[5]

Sadly, the focus on the economic failure of VESC has failed to highlight the tremendous accomplishments of the conservation side of the program. Over the last thirty years the program has protected fourteen barrier islands, major deepwater ports, and mainland buffers, totaling more than forty-five thousand acres of protected area. These efforts have made a permanent positive mark on the future of this important landscape.

VESC was not the only large-scale attempt looking for ways to link compatible development with the environment in the 1990s. In fact, it was not even the most ambitious. For seven years U.S. AID's Biodiversity Conservation Network (BCN) applied the concept of enterprise development and conservation to develop twenty projects in seven countries in Asia and the Pacific. These projects spawned forty-eight community-based enterprises at a cost of $20 million of taxpayer money. Beginning in the late 1980s, BCN selected twenty widely diverse projects: marketing essential oils from Nepal; developing small scale tropical timber business in Gunung Palung, Indonesia; and developing local fishing industries in the Arnovon Islands of Solomon Islands. Still other efforts included butterfly farming, honey raising, and rafting in Lore Lindu National Park, Indonesia.[6]

Although the enterprises were typically smaller than those of VESC, they faced the same issues. Potentially interesting and viable business concepts struggled with one or more fatal flaws in their business plans. In the Arnovon Islands, the conservation goal was to entice local islanders toward plentiful offshore fisheries and away from harvesting turtles and exploitation of near-shore reefs. Fishing equipment, boats, training, and ice plants were all part of the strategy to develop local enterprises to pull fishermen away from endangered resources. But extraneous circumstances plagued the efforts. Plenty of fish were available to be caught and markets were willing to pay a premium for the fish, but delivering fresh fish from a remote island in the South Pacific to markets in Australia, Hawaii, or

Japan proved too daunting a task. First, the fish had to be transported by boat to the capital island—a day's journey—and then connect with weekly flights to Australia for on-shipping to markets. And with a suffering Solomon economy and nearly constant civil strife disrupting airport and boat schedules, it was always uncertain whether the product could get to market in time to meet the high standard of freshness required.

In Lore Lindu National Park in Indonesia, despite efforts to attract rafting companies to the river that forms one boundary of the park, only one trip ever materialized. Logistics, civil conditions that discouraged tourism, and the availability of much more attractive rafting spots undermined any potential for success. And butterfly growing, while apparently economically feasible, floundered for lack of ability to get export licenses amid chaotic civil conditions and corrupt government officials.

In other projects funded by BCN, guest houses were built for tourists, but with no marketing or in some cases even roads to get to the sites, only an few intrepid travelers found their way to the facilities. Training local villages to cater to ecotourists and derive income from nonconsumptive uses of the rainforest is a good idea, but only if visitors actually come.

In spite of the failures, not all results were negative. Engaging local communities in a conservation project brought some excellent on-the-ground results. It appears that working together on the business translated indirectly into stronger communities. Even if the business collapsed or failed to generate cash benefits, the education and awareness created through the effort seemed to pay some dividends to conservation. BCN concluded that "You can't expect any one conservation strategy to save the rainforests and reefs by themselves. Instead, any given project needs to have the appropriate mixture of strategies tailored to meet local conditions."[7] This is an important reminder that engaging the community matters and fostering strong communities may be more durable than any economic enterprise.

My first assignment for TNC in 1996 was working in Papua New Guinea, where we also experimented rather unsuccessfully with compatible development strategies. In early 1996, the government was in the process of expanding logging concessions to include hundreds of thousands of acres of forests. The national park system was woefully inadequate and logging concessions often overlaid these paper parks. With civil war ongoing in parts of the country and collapsing income from the mining industry, the government was desperate to increase revenues to meet very real human needs. A drought, brought on by an unusual combination of warm ocean temperatures, made even the normally verdant highlands, the breadbasket of the country, fire-scarred and unproductive. Despite these enormous challenges, the country is one of the world's most important repositories of biodiversity and unique human culture. With nearly eight hundred languages spoken in a country of 4 million people the communities are as colorful and diverse as the over thirty species of birds of paradise that inhabit the island.

Our strategy was to bid for the logging rights offered by the government on some of the forest concessions in the most biodiverse areas in an effort to ward off the devastating cut-and-run logging operations that prevailed in the country. We hoped that given a sustainable alternative vision for these lands, the country might be enticed into changing their practices. At the same time, TNC had little expertise in sustainable forestry and our success would only be possible if we could partner with a compatible for-profit company. Finding such a business partner proved a difficult assignment. None of the major North American forest product companies had any interest in Papua New Guinea, having largely abandoned efforts to develop mills and forest operations in Asia years before. Weyerhaeuser, for example, was far from encouraging. It had owned a major mill and forest operation in Malaysia, but could not compete in the corruption-dominated environment. The company pulled out at a huge loss.

We finally settled on a small start-up venture, with a single operation in Paraguay as our partner, and before long we found ourselves as the leading contender for a large concession in the Josephstall area along the north coast of Madang Province. However, instability in another part of the world soon obliterated our hopes. The market for tropical logs collapsed because of the deepening economic crisis in Japan—the leading buyer of wood from this area—and the World Bank, in a rare moment of conscience announced that it would suspend economic aid to Papua New Guinea if it did not stop unsustainable logging.

The resulting economic situation and political moratorium effectively killed our efforts. With low log prices we could not compete with rapacious loggers; our venture required us to invest in reduced-impact logging techniques, proper roads, local processing, and training for Papua New Guineans. Even if the venture were economic, for political reasons we could not undermine the World Bank's policy efforts by pressing forward in the face of their moratorium. So although a sustainable forest project would have been a great conservation strategy, three years of effort demonstrated that it was not a viable one despite our earnest wishes to the contrary.

This was not the end of our efforts however. As we came to know the people of the region, we began to appreciate that their interest was not necessarily in logging but in finding modest incomes that would sustain their communities and provide for basic human needs. This opened the door to considering some new ideas. In South America, Conservation International was engaged in pioneering a new concept, "conservation concessions," in which the objective was to lease land from owners or the government for the purposes of conservation and not extraction. With low land prices in Papua New Guinea this concept was potentially feasible but national laws prevented landowners from entering into agreements regarding land use without central government approval. With a logging concession already being promoted by this same government, it took a

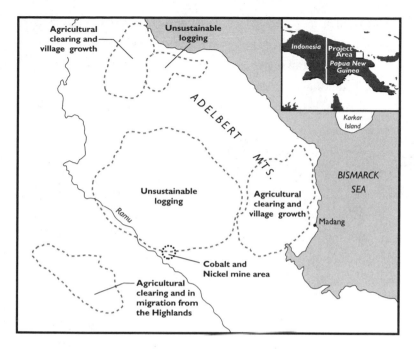

Figure 10.2

Major threats to the forests of Josephstall-Madang Province, Papua New Guinea

further two years to win high court approval to end the concession and pass new legislation explicitly allowing local communities to set aside land for conservation without central government approval. With these legal challenges behind, the project is evolving into an exciting new effort to develop locally controlled management areas that honor community ownership while planning for sustainable uses such as tourism and small-scale agriculture and forestry. The future of the biodiversity of Papua New Guinea is far from certain, but new market based models are emerging from the failures of previous efforts particularly suited to those countries with traditional patterns of community land ownership.

So what lessons can we learn from Virginia, Papua New Guinea, and Indonesia? First it is clear that conservation organizations need to recognize what they are good at and not good at. Developing and managing businesses is usually not a core competency for conservation organizations—although there may be exceptions. For example, the Appalachian Mountain Club has proven itself an effective operator of a sizable backcountry recreational business and the successful manager of a string of eco-lodges and nature-oriented facilities throughout the northeast. Arguably, this *is* their core competency.

Secondly, just because a business idea would be good for conservation, does not necessarily mean that it is a viable, profitable business venture. Any business that tries to achieve the "triple" bottom line implied by sustainability—economics, environment, and equity—faces a daunting task, even with a strong entrepreneur at the helm. Again and again these ventures have demonstrated that simply investing in a conservation business concept will not guarantee paying customers or a profitable future.

Although success has been elusive, the concept of compatible economic development is still worth pursuing. In spite of failures, the effort to move toward an economic environment that favors sustainability is still central to our future. Success, however, will most often be achieved by partnering with others—community development groups that specialize in micro-enterprises, entrepreneurs with proven business expertise and conservation capital, or the creation of incentives—regulatory and/or financial—that favor conservation-oriented business ventures over their unsustainable competitors.

Box 10.1

Lessons about Compatible Development

Key lessons learned from conservation groups engaging in compatible development:

A good move for conservation is not necessarily a profitable business move. Test your ideas thoroughly and make sure that a conservationist's ideology is not substituting for sound economic judgment.

Beware the law of unintended consequences—compatible economic development may create as many problems as it solves. Economic systems and markets are messy and they don't follow conservation rules.

Stick to the knitting. Most conservation groups lack the core competencies to run businesses. The nonprofit culture is a different environment than business entrepreneurship.

Partnerships with businesses may be a better alternative than direct engagement in business ventures. Conservation groups can and should work to provide missing ingredients in their business plan—capital, technical support, political efforts, and policy environments that favor sustainable enterprises.

11

Conservation at the Scale of Nature

Many of us have a dream for the Northern Forest. My dream is that we will preserve the beauty and wildness of this great land while protecting respectful
human participation in the landscape for generations to come.

—Stephen Gorman, *Northeastern Wilds*

Since 1999, I've been working for The Nature Conservancy (TNC) in the
Northern Appalachian eco-region, an 80-million-acre stretch of largely
undeveloped and intact forest that connects two countries—Canada and
the United States—into a single forest.[1] Stretching from the Canadian
Maritimes to New York's Adirondacks, the northern end of the glaciated
and weathered Appalachian Mountains runs through the landscape. The
region is a lush and diverse setting of mostly northern hardwood and
spruce-fir forests, remarkably intact despite its proximity to major cities
in Canada and the United States.

This was a landscape settled early by white explorers, and it bears the
mark of three hundred years of timber harvesting and human use. Unlike
the West, it is largely privately owned in the United States with the notable
exceptions of the Adirondack Forest Preserve and two modest-sized national forests. In Canada, while private ownership is still a major force,
Crown ownership dominates much of the forested areas. Yet even in these
publicly owned areas, long-term leases to private forest companies are the

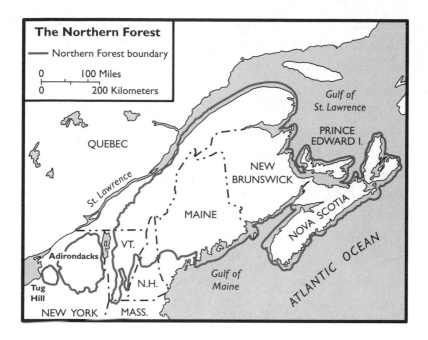

Figure 11.1

The Northern Forest

normal management strategy. The long history of use by private companies and the relatively good condition of the landscape testify to an underlying theme of this book. Landowners can be effective guardians of the land given the right incentives. And, in this landscape, the economic forces shaping the region for several hundred years have favored simply growing trees and lots of them.

Change is afoot in the landscape, though. After almost one hundred years of stable private ownership the region has undergone rapid churning of land tenure. In Maine, over one third of the entire state, 7 million acres, has been bought and sold in the last five years. The latest sale of 1.1 million acres of International Paper (IP) lands covers 5 percent of the state alone. In New Hampshire, another IP sale resulted in nearly 4 percent of the state being sold. Even in eastern Canada, Domtar Company of Quebec has announced plans to divest itself of over 1 million acres to pay down debt and focus on its paper manufacturing business.

Despite the dominant private ownership, the region had some magnificent early conservation successes—most notably Governor Percival Baxter's acquisition of two hundred thousand acres of Maine wilderness that now bears his name, the creation of the White and Green Mountain National Forests, and, of course, the Adirondack Forest Preserve. Still, conservation had lain fallow for many decades until the early 1990s when a new round of conservation work began to transform much of the region.

Early on, the conservation community came to the conclusion that the principal conservation goal needed to be protection of the rich forest matrix of the region. This is not a land where a single charismatic creature, such as the wolf or grizzly bear, still dominates the system. Instead, the patchwork of ecological communities forming the Northern Forest favors dozens of types of neotropical warblers and songbirds as well as smaller mammals, such as the fisher, pine marten, lynx, and bobcat. The substantial Hudson, Connecticut, Penobscot, and St. John rivers bisect the region, and mill-dependent hamlets dot the cultural and economic landscape. Working to protect the overarching forest matrix by keeping those systems intact has become the major focus of modern conservation efforts in the region.

A legacy of private stewardship has done a pretty good job keeping the system intact and functioning. Many, although not all, of the region's species seem comfortable in the historic system of long rotation, natural forest management. This system, however, is undergoing dramatic revision by new economic forces. Fifty million people on the East Coast, lured by thousands of undeveloped lakes and miles of rivers within a day's drive, are beginning to create development pressure on the forests. Also, in order to compete, the new industrial owners are practicing much more aggressive silviculture along the thousands of miles of access roads that spider

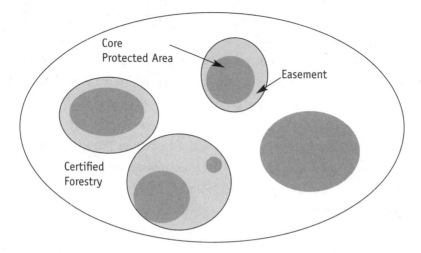

Figure 11.2

Northern Forest Biodiversity Strategy (Source: Anderson, "N-dimensional Pinball." Used by permission.)

through the forest, replacing the historic log drives on the many small rivers of the region. Finally, nature produced its impact as well, with a periodic spruce budworm epidemic in the mid-1970s devastating millions of acres and thus further undermining the economic incentive to keep forestland as forestland.

With millions of acres at risk and limited philanthropic and public dollars, the conservationists working in this region began to realize that a practical set of new strategies would be necessary. A vision for the future of this region began to emerge based on "right-sized" core reserves protected by buffers of eased working forest where conservation easements limit development and require sustainable management. These legally protected areas would be imbedded in areas conserved though voluntary, cooperative efforts between with landowners, their customers, and local communities. To achieve this new approach, conservationists needed to demonstrate to forestland owners the benefits of forest certification and large-scale conservation easements and to find the resources to create a network of carefully selected reserves.

Selecting the right forest areas to conserve and to match these with the appropriate level of protection spawned new thinking about prioritization and conservation design. Led by Dr. Mark Anderson, TNC's director of science in the northeast, new analytical tools emerged. The concept of "ecological land units" provided one clue to selecting the right areas to focus on. Intact blocks of forestland were mapped across the region and then analyzed for key geophysical attributes. This effort enabled conservation planners to distinguish forest blocks dominated by granitic mastiffs, such as those of the White Mountains, from the calcareous soils of Vermont's Champlain Valley and Maine's Aroostook County. Each of these distinct forest matrix types supports a unique combination of forest, plant, and wildlife species. In the end nine basic types of forest communities, representing a high percentage of the biodiversity of the forest, were identified across the region.

To protect multiple examples of these nine types of forests across the region with appropriate buffer zones of working forest is a sobering undertaking. Priority forest matrix sites potentially spanned nearly 6 million acres on the U.S. side alone. The prevailing question was, How much of these forest sites really needed protection and at what level? Again, Mark Anderson's team provided some critical answers. They began by analyzing historic patterns of disturbance from natural causes, such as fire, windstorms, and hurricanes. If protected areas were too small they would be subject to potential catastrophic disturbances that would potentially wipe out generations of efforts to create old-growth conditions. The region has some stark examples of this. In Connecticut one of the last remaining old-growth areas of some three hundred acres was blown down in seconds by a tornado. Clearly three-hundred-acre old-growth sites were not enough to ensure that viable old-growth systems were maintained. Another factor to be considered was the minimum area of old-growth forest required to ensure the survival of key species. In this case the scientific consensus was that protecting enough land to have at least twenty-five breeding pairs of key species was essential to have a viable population in the reserve area. Since not all species thrive in old growth conditions—lynx, fisher, bobcats, and wolves are reasonably comfortable in working forest areas—the focus was on neotropical bird migrants, northern goshawks and pine marten, all of which need old-growth conditions to thrive and whose presence is a strong indication of the overall ecological health of the protected area. In the end the scientists settled on a goal of at least twenty-five thousand acres in each of the identified examples of forest matrix areas. Ideally these would be surrounded by a buffer of sustainably managed forests protected by easements and voluntary certification efforts. There are no absolute guidelines in setting these goal: bigger buffer areas of protected working forest may mean that a particular reserve can be smaller and still be effective and conversely, a protected area that is surrounded by development needs to be much bigger to achieve its ecological goals. It is also clear that whatever the minimum, bigger is better when it comes to protected areas.

As this vision emerged, other scientists contributed significant thinking about connecting areas of forest blocks in order to ensure that wideranging species, such as lynx, can move freely between matrix areas, and someday perhaps even the historically present but extirpated eastern timber wolf might reappear from across the St. Lawrence River into the region. Although not universally supported by the conservation community, especially those seeking a national park as their ultimate aspiration, many agree that this plan, at the very least, protects a lot of biodiversity and buys time for the future.

For the plan to work conservationists needed to implement both traditional strategies like buying adequate parks and reserves as well as ensure the viability of the working forest in the buffer areas. Coincidentally, this vision closely mirrors the emerging global goal of setting aside 10 to

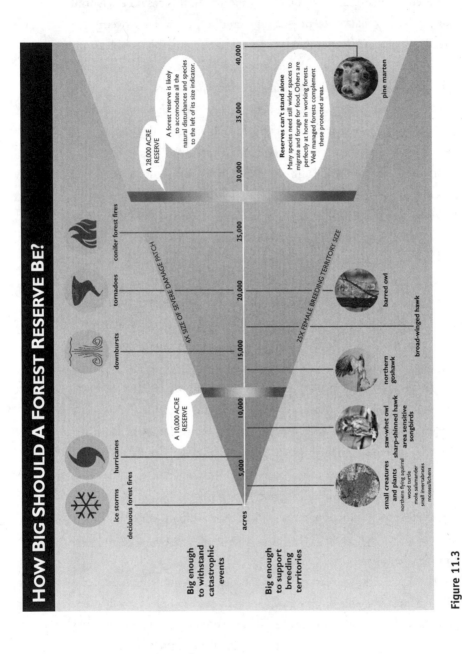

Figure 11.3

Scaling Factors for Reserves in the Northern Forest

15 percent of the world's surface area for biodiversity management embedded in the sustainable management of the remaining 85 percent of the landscape.

Since the 1990s a great deal has been accomplished to implement this vision. Two million acres of forest easements to create critical buffers have been put in place. Five hundred thousand acres of new reserves have been acquired and nearly 8 million acres of forestland have been certified. Over $100 million of private equity capital has matched nearly $200 million of philanthropic and government funds to achieve this result. A new architecture of ownership and protection is slowly emerging across the landscape.

Nowhere have new strategies been more effectively implemented than in the tristate area of northern Vermont, New Hampshire, and western Maine. In 1990, very few of the priority sites had protection outside of the White Mountain National Forest. Nearly fifteen years of steady progress have redefined this region's appearance. Innovative marketplace tools and traditional common sense conservation have guided the process. Private deals with investors allowed conservation to gain footholds as IP and Champion retrenched in the region, spawning landmark conservation transactions with private investors in northern New Hampshire and Vermont. These partnerships with private investors have protected over three hundred thousand acres of working forests and ensured the creation of core reserves on another ninety thousand acres.

Other forces were also at work shaping the future of this tristate area. First, a well-respected long-term landowner, the Pingree family, bucked the trend of divestiture and, instead, sold a conservation easement on 750,000 acres of land in Maine to the New England Forestry Foundation. Second, a series of exciting new transaction types began to occur. US Gen, holder of hydro rights and dams on the Connecticut River, announced that as part of its relicensing efforts, they would be granting a twenty-three-thousand-acre easement on key riparian corridors along

Box 11.1

Major Land Conservation Transactions—Vermont, New Hampshire, and Western Maine

Partnerships with Private Investors

Champion, VT: 147,000 acres protected, including 90,000 acres now owned by Essex Timber and subject to a working forest easement. Critical reserves protected by Conti National Wildlife Refuge and State of Vermont.

Bunnell Tract, NH: Eighteen thousand acres protected, including nine thousand acres subject to an easement in partnership with GMO Renewable Resources. Reserves held by TNC.

IP Connecticut Lakes: 171,000 acres protected, including 25,000 acres of reserves now owned by state of NH and 142,000 acres owned by Lyme Timber subject to an easement.

Valuing Water Resources for Conservation

Rangeley Lakes: $1 million for land conservation by Florida Power and Light as part of FERC relicensing proceedings.

Connecticut Headwater Lakes in NH and VT: Easement on twenty-three thousand acres of riparian corridor of Connecticut River and headwater lakes by US GEN as part of FERC proceedings.

Customer Demand For Greener Products

Sustainable Forest Initiative Certification: 500,000 acres of MeadWestvaco lands (now managed by Wagner), 1.1 million acres of International Paper Company lands (now owned by GMO), among others.

Forest Stewardship Council Certification: 500,000 acres of Maine Public Reserve lands and 1 million acres of land managed by Seven Islands Land Company.

Working Forest Easements

Pingree Family, ME: 750,000 acres covered by a working forest easement
throughout Maine.

Traditional Purchases:

Nash State Forest, NH: forty-seven thousand acres purchased by TNC for the
state of NH.
Community Forests, NH: Town of Randolph, NH, five thousand acres.
Expansion of Umbagog National Wildlife Refuge, NH and ME: twenty thou-
sand acres.
Appalachian Trail protection: twenty-five thousand acres.

Connecticut's Vermont and New Hampshire shores. A similar deal in
Maine in the Rangeley Lakes grew out of the efforts of Florida Power and
Light (FPL) to relicense dams in that region. The company agreed to award
nearly $1 million to the Rangeley Lakes Land Trust for land-acquisition
efforts that would allow the group to complete much of the work already
started by an earlier gift of eight thousand acres of land from a local
landowner on the shores of several of Rangeley's major lakes.

Finally, certification began to make its mark across the region, with
major landowners signing on in rapid succession. For the Pingree- and
state-owned land in Maine, dual certification by both Sustainable Forest
Initiative (SFI) and Forest Stewardship Council (FSC) was chosen; for IP
and Mead-Westvaco, SFI certification alone was implemented.

With these and dozens of other smaller transactions, the region's conservation overlay has evolved in fifteen years, as shown in figure 11.4.

This present condition is not a pretty picture of success but a messy
layering of different strategies and different levels of protection. Taken

singly, any of these strategies would fail to achieve the scale of conservation required in the region. But taken as a whole and linked together, the result is nothing short of impressive. Within our priority conservation sites in this area of the Northern Forest alone, 873,000 acres of all types of terrain have some level of protection—over 60 percent of the conservation goal. Counting the opportunities that have spilled beyond the borders of this particular area, the total protected landscape pushes 1.3 million acres in this portion of the Northern Forest. Overall, this is a solution that seeks to honor both biodiversity and wilderness while accepting the importance of people who live and work in this landscape. Nurturing this fragile coalition between communities, industry, and conservationists is a long-term challenge that will be critical to our success. As noted conservation commentator Scott Russell Sanders has pointed out, "No matter what the legal protections on the ground, no land will be safe from harm without people committed to caring for it, year after year, generation after generation. All conservation must therefore aim at fostering an ethic of stewardship."[2]

Our work is not done. Climate change, invasive species, and atmospheric deposition all threaten the region, and no amount of local effort or land protection will solve these global threats. Secondly, many of our conservation targets are protected only by voluntary arrangements like certification that might not survive a corporate or private land change. Community support for these initiatives fluctuates as the economic winds of mill shutdowns and start-ups sweep the region. Change is hard for many of these areas where a hundred years of consistent ownership is upset by land sales and development. But we believe that we are headed in the right direction.

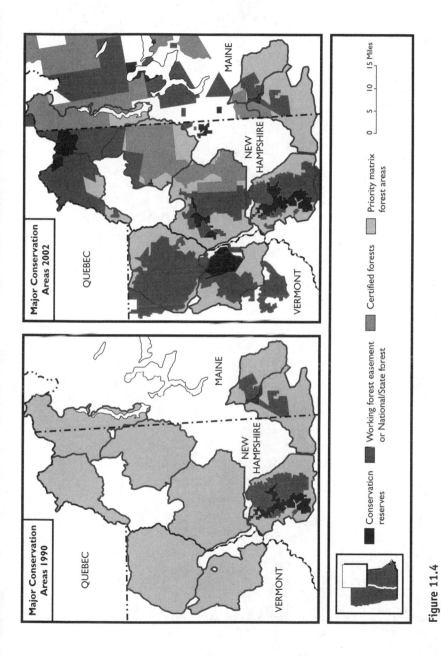

Figure 11.4

Major Conservation Projects, 1990 and 2002 (Source: Adapted from Anderson, "N-dimensional Pinball." Used by permission.)

Box 11.2

Northern Forest Resources

Northern Forest Alliance

George Gay, executive director

43 State St.

Montpelier, VT 05602

Phone: 802-223-5256, ext. 11

Fax: 802-229-4642

Website: www.northernforestalliance.org

This group focuses on policy work on the U.S. side of the Northern Forest and has been engaged for ten years in defining a vision for the region.

Northern Forest Center

Steve Blackmere, president

P.O. Box 210

18 North Main St., Suite 302

Concord, NH 03302-0210

Phone: 603-229-0679

Fax: 603-229-1719

Website:www.northernforest.org

The Center is engaged in keeping the vision of traditional culture and land use alive in the region.

Two Countries, One Forest

6151 Allan St.

Halifax NS B3L 1G7

Canada

Phone: 902-422-2005

James Sullivan, Executive Director, sullivan@web.net

A network of U.S. and Canadian groups seeking to work together to create a long-term ecologically viable landscape.

12

Crossing the Divide

The Great Work now, as we move into a new millennium, is to carry out the transition from a period of human devastation of the Earth to a period when humans would be present to the planet in a mutually beneficial manner.

—Thomas Berry, *The Great Work*

In a world where capitalism dominates so much of our cultural and political landscape, harnessing and redirecting its forces makes practical sense. With most countries struggling to protect even 10 percent of their landmass, we can't afford to ignore the remaining landscape, the important ecological functions it provides, and the communities that are part of it. "Conservationists," says Scott Sanders, "have much to learn from people who still draw sustenance from the land —hunting, fishing farming, ranching, gardening, logging. The most thoughtful of these people use the land respectfully, for they understand the earth is the ultimate source of wealth."[1] Applying market-oriented tools to help move more people and businesses toward the goal of a sustainable world may be the best hope we have. As Paul Hawkins has observed, "Ironically, business contains our blessing. It must, because no other institution in the modern world is powerful enough to foster the necessary changes."[2] And, as he also contends, "No 'plan' to reverse environmental degradation can be enacted if it requires a wholesale change in the dynamics of the market."[3]

If I had been told as a youth that my conservation efforts would thrust me into complex business deals in corporate boardrooms, I would have been aghast. My world then was dominated by idealism and an uncompromising love of wilderness in its purest form. Now, thirty-odd years into my adult life, I hope I have not lost any of my early commitment to conservation, but I have come to appreciate the potential of a new set of pragmatic tools aimed squarely at achieving a world where the human community rests comfortably and compatibly within natural communities that reflect the diversity of life on earth.

Clearly reserves, national parks, and wilderness need our continued vigilance and support. Much of this will need to be accomplished with traditional land conservation tools. But the whooping crane, the Kirkland warbler, and the trumpeter swan cannot exist on nesting reserves and winter-protected areas alone. All must migrate every year across a landscape occupied by people, and favorable conditions on working ranches and forests along the way are necessary for their survival. The good news is that countless farmers and foresters along the way wish them well and support their right to be part of the land.

There is no going back to a world where nature, absent of any human impact, rules the day. As Michael Pollan points out, "Even Yellowstone, our country's greatest 'wilderness' stands in need of careful management—it's too late to simply 'leave it alone.' Today, even Yellowstone must be 'gardened.'"[4] Managing our interactions with natural systems will not be easy, nor will the answers always be clear, but manage we must; no other approach offers a future for people in the global ecological equation.

The expectations on governments to ensure the conservation of biodiversity are significant. In fact, the Convention of Biodiversity, signed by almost all of the world's countries (except, sadly, the United States), commits the world to setting aside a fully representative protected areas system covering at least 10 percent of the globe before 2015. Yet even if governments achieve this conservation goal, nature doesn't function within neat lines of demarcation, and reserves will be inadequate if development has paved up to the doors of the sanctuary. The St. John needs its ice to scour the banks to create fertile ground for the lousewort. Only a world that manages its climate balance by keeping consumption of resources in check can maintain those conditions in place. Our forests can provide a portion of the answers, for wood is a remarkable building material: renewable, recyclable. Sustainably managed, forests can be the backbone of our housing and, in much of the world, fuel for heating and cooking; or their potential can be squandered by poor management and illegal harvesting. This fate will force us ever more deeply into a world of synthetics and unsustainable, energy-intensive substitutes.

Because many of the challenges that face us are linked to commerce, the engagement of communities will be essential. One of the most distinguishing features of the human species is our ability to collaborate. The economy is one tangible manifestation of this highly evolved system of cooperation. This places working with people at the center of our strategies. Market-oriented tools will be essential strategies toward creating this new vision for sustainable use of resources. But this still may not be enough, for as Peter Forbes has observed, "This aspiration for land conservation will not be reached alone by how much how much nature we can put aside, but by how much love and respect for the land we can engender in the greatest number of people."[5] Neglecting the "why" we are doing our work will diminish our chances for success just as surely as failing to see the advantage of working with the powerful forces of the marketplace.

A broader vision, as espoused by the Earth Charter, for example, recognizes that natural areas, as important as they may be, will be insufficient if we fail to address other fundamental issues.[6] Social and economic justice, democracy, nonviolence, and peace are integral to achieving ecological integrity. The change in values and direction necessary will require a far bolder vision of working to build communities, eradicate poverty, and sustainably use our resources if we are to have any hope of preserving life on earth. And I contend that integrating conservation into the market-place will be central to this transformation.

Change will not come easily. Back in 1927, Governor Baxter's plan to protect Mt. Katahdin met with derision from the Maine press. "The silliest proposal ever made to a Legislature was that of Governor Baxter who advocated the State's buying Mount Katahdin and creating a State Park," proclaimed the *Portland Press Herald.*[7] In the end, Baxter pressed forward with his own personal fortune to acquire what is now revered as one of the most inspiring conservation achievements of the twentieth century. As we chart our course forward, we will face similar challenges but the summit looms ahead.

To achieve success, the incentives that direct our economy will need to push our rafts in the direction of the right shoreline. If poverty dominates many of the world's biodiversity hot spots or if consumers are indifferent to the source of their purchases, the incentives to cut too much, to intensify our farming, to overburden our land will be overwhelming. If, on the other hand, a global commitment to sustainability becomes the standard for the way trees are harvested, farms are managed, and communities supported, then there is hope for all. Commerce is a formidable force with no inherent environmental conscience driving it. Only we can shape its direction. Understanding the nature *of* business may be the best tool we have to put nature *in* business. Crossing this divide is the great work ahead.

Notes

Introduction: The Scale of Nature

1. For many helpful and alarming statistics about the economy including information on housing trends see: www.economicindicators.gov/.

2. Wade Rawlins, "N.C. Forests Falling Fast: State Lost More Than 1 Million Acres from 1990 to 2002," *North Carolina News and Observer*, March 26, 2004.

3. The official site of the U.S. government covering macroeconomic trends can be found at www.bea.gov.

4. "An Environmental Deficit," *New York Times*, editorial, February 11, 2004.

5. E. O. Wilson, *The Future of Life* (New York: Knopf, 2002), 156.

Chapter 1: Partnering with Big Timber

1. Peter Forbes, Kathleen D. Moore, and Scott R. Sanders. *Coming to Land in a Troubled World* (San Francisco: The Trust For Public Lands, 2004), xii.

2. *Timberland Markets* (North Hollywood, CA: Paperloop 1:6 December 2003).

3. Ibid.

4. Ibid.

Chapter 3: Bankruptcy and Biodiversity

1. For a detailed discussion of many issues related to forest management and the Trillium project in particular see David Lindenmayer, and Jerry Franklin, *Conserving Forest Biodiversity* (Washington, D.C.: Island Press, 2002).

2. "Goldman Sachs to Create Nature Reserve in Southern Chile," Press Release from Goldman Sachs, December 12, 2003.

Chapter 4: Investing with an Attitude

1. Marsha Glickman and Marjorie Kelly, "Working Capital," *E Magazine*, March-April, 2004, 28–34.

2. *2003 Report on Socially Responsible Investing Trends in the US* (Washington, D.C.: Social Investment Forum, 2003).

Chapter 5: Carbon and Forests

1. Sandra Postal and Brian Richter, *Rivers for Life: Managing Water for People and Nature* (Washington, D.C.: Island Press, 2004), 6–7.

2. From a press release issued by The Nature Conservancy available at http://nature.org/pressroom/press/press985.html.

3. Attributed to Steve McCormick, president, The Nature Conservancy, and available at http://34568.portal.tnc.org/xa/cfp/diversity/index.html.

4. "California Leads on Warming," *New York Times*, op. ed., June 15, 2004.

5. "Agriculture and Forestry Greenhouse Gas Baseline and Reduction Options," *Maine Greenhouse Action Plan*, revised June 18, 2004, 10–12.

6. "Forest Carbon in the United States," *Pacific Forests* 3-2 (2000): 4.

7. "Carbon Solution: How More Forests Can Mean Less Warming," *Pacific Forests* 7–1 (Spring 2004): 4.

8. "Forest Carbon in the United States," *Pacific Forests* 3-2 (2000):3–5.

Chapter 6: The Bank of Nature

1. W. DeBuys, *Valle Grande Grass Bank: The Case Study* (Virginia: The Conservation Fund, 1999), unpublished.

2. Verlyn Klinkenborg, "Crossing Borders," *Audubon* (Sept./Oct. 1995):128.

3. Ibid., 128–129.

4. Hal Herring, "Fair Trade Ranchers Bank on Conservation," *Nature Conservancy* Spring (2004):20–21.

5. Ibid., 20.

6. Heart Mt. Grassbank, Business Plan (Arlington: The Nature Conservancy, December 2002), unpublished.

7. Terry L. Anderson and Donald R. Leal. *Enviro-Capitalists: Doing Well While Doing Good* (Lanham: Rowman and Littlefield, 1997), 94.

8. Ibid., 96.

9. "Alcoa Willing to Swap Land for New Dam License," Associated Press, April 20, 2004.

Chapter 7: Greening Business

1. Information about The Nature Conservancy's efforts in Indonesia came from: Nigel Sizer, "How Can TNC Combat Illegal Logging in Indonesia?" A presentation at the Forest Strategies Conference, Arlington, Virginia, June 2003.

2. As reported in an article by Jonathan Hopfner, in *BNA*, an Indonesian newspaper on January 21, 2004.

3. Ibid.

4. From remarks delivered by Jim Hill of Mead Westvaco at the Who Will Own the Forest? conference, Portland, Oregon, September 22, 2004.

5. From a presentation by J. Refkin at the Governor's Natural Resources Conference, Maine, December 2003. A copy of the presentation is available at www.maine.gov/governors/baldacci/news/events/refkin_files.

6. As reported on the Time, Inc. company website in "Friend of the Earth," http://infocenter.aoltw.com.

7. For this and current information on this project I recommend www.savethegreatbear.org.

8. Stephen Gorman, *Northeastern Wilds* (Boston: Appalachian Mountain Club Books, 2002), 168.

Chapter 8: Tax Credits for Conservation

1. I am greatly indebted to the work of Phil Tabas, general counsel for The Nature Conservancy for sharing his extensive knowledge of this material for this chapter.

2. News item from *Common Ground* 15, 2 (April-June 2004):4.

3. As stated in the company's web site: www.aquarion.com/recreation.html, accessed April 21, 2004.

Chapter 9: Incentives for Working Landscapes

1. Attributed to Wilcove et al., 1996, as reported in Edwin G. Sauls, "Practical Tips for Developers," *Developers Guide to Endangered Species Regulation* (Washington, D.C.: National Homebuilders Association, 1996), 109.

2. *Progress on the Back Forty* (Washington, D.C.: Environmental Defense Fund, 2000), 7.

3. William Weeks, *Beyond the Ark* (Washington, D.C.: Island Press, 1997), 142.

4. Terry Karkos, "Federal Money to Help Preserve Wildlife Habitat," Sun Journal (Lewiston, Maine), March 4, 2004.

5. "LIP Program Highlights Struggle over Which Species Need Help," *Land Letter*, March 11, 2003.

6. *Progress on the Back Forty*, 18.

Chapter 10: If You Build It, Will They Come?

1. Brian Dabson, Peter Plastrick, and Richard Turner, *Lessons from the Life and Death of the Virginia Eastern Shore Corporation* (Washington, D.C.: Corporation for Enterprise Development, Spring 2001), 7.

2. Ibid., 7.

3. William Weeks, *Beyond the Ark*, (Washington, D.C.: Island Press, 1997), 93.

4. *Virginia Coast Reserve Program Assessment—August 2002, Final Report* (Arlington, VA: The Nature Conservancy, 2002), unpublished.

5. Ibid.

6. Nick Salafsky et al., *Evaluating Linkages between Business and the Environment and Local Communities* (Washington, D.C.: Biodiversity Support Program, 1999).

7. Ibid.

Chapter 11: Conservation at the Scale of Nature

1. The intellectual brainpower for much of the eco-regional planning and conservation concepts in this chapter come from Dr. Mark Anderson, Director of Science for TNC's Northeastern Division and developed as part of TNC's Northern Appalachian Ecoregional Plan.

2. From Scott Russell Sanders, "Conservationist's Manifesto," in Peter Forbes, Kathleen D. Moore, and Scott R. Sanders, *Coming to Land in a Troubled World* (San Francisco: The Trust for Public Lands, 2004), 21.

Chapter 12: Crossing the Divide

1. Peter Forbes, Kathleen D. Moore, and Scott R. Sanders, *Coming to Land in a Troubled World* (San Francisco: The Trust for Public Lands, 2004), 23.

2. Paul Hawkins, *The Ecology of Commerce* (New York: Harper Business, 1993), 17.

3. Ibid., xv.

4. From Michael Pollan, *Second Nature* (1991) as quoted in Peter Forbes, Ann Forbes, and Helen Whybrow, eds., *Our Land, Ourselves, Readings on People and Place* (San Francisco: Trust for Public Lands, 1999), 97.

5. Peter Forbes, *The Great Remembering: Further Thoughts on Land, Soul and Society* (San Francisco: Trust for Public Lands, 2001), 84.

6. For a full discussion of the Earth Charter see www.earthcharter.org.

7. Neil Rolde, *The Baxter's of Maine* (Gardner, ME: Tilbury House, 1997), 222.

Bibliography

"Agriculture and Forestry Greenhouse Gas Baseline and Reduction Options." *Maine Greenhouse Action Plan.* Revised June 18, 2004.

Agriculture and Forestry Working Group, State of Maine. *Report to Stakeholders from the Agriculture and Forestry Working Group.* July 21, 2004.

"Alcoa Willing to Swap Land for New Dam License." Associated Press, April 20, 2004.

AMC White Mountain Guide 25th Edition. Boston: Appalachian Mountain Club, 1992.

Anderson, Mark. "N–dimension Pinball." Unpublished powerpoint presentation given at Two Countries, One Forest Conference, Montreal, 2004.

Anderson, Terry L. and Donald R. Leal. *Enviro-Capitalists: Doing Well While Doing Good.* Lanham, MD: Rowman and Littlefield, 1997.

"An Environmental Deficit." *New York Times,* editorial, February 11, 2004.

Aquarion. http://www.aquarion.com/.

Barnes, Peter. *Who Owns the Sky: Our Common Assets and the Future of Capitalism.* Washington, D.C.: Island Press, 2001.

Bergman, Barry. *Pacific Forests.* Santa Rosa, CA: The Pacific Forest Trust, Spring 2004.

Berry, Thomas. *The Great Work, Our Way into the Future.* New York: Bell Tower, 1999.

Berry, Wendell. *Another Turn of the Crank.* Washington, D.C.: Counterpoint Press, 1995.

Birch, Simon. "That's the Spirit." *The Guardian,* August 24, 2002.

Block, Nadine E., and V. Alaric Sample., eds. *Industrial Timberland Divestitures and Investments: Opportunities and Challenges in Forestland Conservation.* Washington, D.C.: Pinchot Institute for Conservation, 2001.

Bridge, Maurice. "Radical Land-use Plan Proposed on Central Coast: Large Areas Will be Set Aside for Grizzlies and Other Wildlife." *The Vancouver Sun*, January 16, 2004, B8.

Bryant, Dirk, Daniel Nielsen, and Laura Tangley. *The Last Frontier Forests: Ecosystems and Economies on the Edge.* World Resources Institute, Forest Frontiers Initiative, 1997.

Butler, Tom., ed. *Wild Earth: The Journal of the Wildlands Project.* Richmond, VA: The Wildlands Project, Spring/Summer 2004.

"California Leads on Warming." *New York Times*, editorial, June 15, 2004.

Canadian Boreal Initiative. "Forest Industry Takes Step toward Boreal Conservation." Press release, Montreal, January 26, 2004.

———. "Industry, First Nations and Conservationists Join Forces behind Largest Conservation Vision in Canadian History." Press release, Ottawa, December 1, 2003. *Canada's Boreal Forest: A Global Opportunity.* Ottawa Ont: CPAWS, March 2004.

"Carbon Solution: How More Forests Can Mean Less Warming." *Pacific Forest.* Santa Rosa: Pacific Forest Trust, Spring 2004.

Carey, John. "Global Warming: Special Report." *Business Week*, August 16, 2004.

Carroll, Carlos. *Special Paper Number 5. Impacts of Landscape Change on Wolf Viability in the Northeastern US and Southeastern Canada; Implications for Wolf Recovery.* Richmond, VT: Wildlands Project, 2003.

The Center for Whole Communities. *Measures of Health: Describing and Measuring the Connection Between Land and People—Version 4.0*, 2004.

Chu, Showwei. "Chance to See White Spirit Bear Divine." *The Globe and Mail*, May 15, 2004.

Coalition for the Permanent Protection of Kelda Lands. *A Crisis Is Brewing in Connecticut Today Brought on by the Potential Sale and Development of Vast Tracts of Open Space by Kelda and other Public Utilities.* Powerpoint presentation.

Connecticut Fund for the Environment. *The Coalition for the Permanent Protection of Kelda Land.* www.cfenc.org.

———. *Kelda CEO Offers Concerns, Cooperation, and a Regional Water Authority.* New Haven, CT. www.cfenv.org.

Coastal Enterprises. *Fishtag Report.* June 2003.

Collins, James C. and Jerry I. Porras. *Built to Last: Successful Habits of Visionary Companies.* New York: HarperCollins, 2002.

Colnes, Andi and Steve Blackmer. *"Community Heritage Enhancement and Enterprise Act for Rural Sustainability"(CHEERS) in the Northern Forest (Draft).* Northern Forest Center, April 19, 2004.

Compatible Ventures. *Grassbanks FAQ.* Accessed from www.compatibleventures.us/grassbank_faq.html, 2003.

Conroy, Michael E., Jose Gabriel Lopez, Camila Moreno, and Mia Charlene White. *Sustainable Solutions: Building Assets for Empowerment and Sustainable Development.* Ford Foundation, August 2002.

"Conservancy, Ranchers Connect for Prairie Chicken." *The Santa Fe New Mexican,* editorial, September 5, 2004.

Conservation Forest Partners and The Nature Conservancy. *Concept Summary and Responses.* February, 2004.

The Conservation Fund. *The Conservation Fund Year in Review 2002.* Arlington, VA, 2002.

————. *Valle Grande Grass Bank: The Case Study.* Available online at http://www.conservationfund.org/pdf/casestudy.pdf. Fall 2004.

Coperthwaite, William. *A Handmade Life: In Search of Simplicity.* White River Junction, VT: Chelsea Green Publishing Company, 2002.

Dabson, Brian, Peter Plastrik, and Richard Turner. *Lessons from the Life and Death of the Virginia Eastern Shore Corporation.* Washington, D.C.: Corporation for Enterprise Development, Spring 2001.

Daily, Gretchen C. and Katherine Ellison. *The New Economy of Nature.* Washington, D.C.: Island Press, 2002.

Daly, Herman E. and Joshua Farley. *Ecological Economics: Principals and Applications.* Washington, D.C.: Island Press, 2004.

Davis, Tim. *Forests for Life: Working to Protect, Manage and Restore the Worlds Forests.* Gland, Switzerland: World Wide Fund for Nature, 2002.

DeBuys, W. *Valle Grande Grass Bank: The Case Study,* Virginia, 1999, unpublished.

Dumanoski, Dianne. "Rethinking Environmentalism," *Conservation Matters,* Fall 1998.

Eddowes, Peter J. *Commercial Timbers of Papua New Guinea: Their Properties and Uses.* Port Moresby: Forest Products Research Centre, 1977.

Ernst, Caryn. *Protecting the Source: Land Conservation and the Future of America's Drinking Water.* San Francisco: The Trust For Public Land, 2004.

Feigenbaum, Cliff, ed. *Green Money Journal,* Spring 2004.

———. *Green Money Journal,* Summer 2004.

———. *Green Money Journal,* Fall 2004.

Forbes, Peter. *The Great Remembering: Further Thoughts on Land, Soul and Society.* San Francisco: The Trust for Public Lands, 2001.

Forbes, Peter, Ann Forbes, and Helen Whybrow, eds. *Our Land, Ourselves, Readings on People and Place.* San Francisco: The Trust for Public Lands, 1999.

Forbes, Peter, Kathleen D. Moore, and Scott R. Sanders. *Coming to Land in a Troubled World.* San Francisco: The Trust For Public Lands, 2004.

"Forest Carbon in the United States." *Pacific Forests.* Santa Rosa: Pacific Forest Trust, 2000.

Freedman, Andrew. "Landowner Incentive Program Highlights Struggle over Which Species Need Help." *Land Letter,* March 11, 2003.

Glickman, Marshall and Marjorie Kelly. "Working Capital." *E Magazine,* March–April 2004.

Goldman Sachs. "Goldman Sachs to Create Nature Reserve in Southern Chile." Press release, December 12, 2003.

Gorman, Stephen. *Northeastern Wilds: Journeys of Discovery in the Northern Forest.* Boston: Appalachian Mountain Club Press, 2002.

Gose, Ben. "Tax and Save: New State Laws Encouraging Landowners to Set Aside Land for Conservation." *The Nature Conservancy Magazine,* Winter 2003.

"Grass Banking." Accessed from www.redlodgeclearinghouse.org/news/grassbanking.html, April 29, 2004.

Grassbanks. Sonoran Institute Glossary. Accessed from www.sonoran.org/resources/terms/si_glossary_grass.html, April 29, 2004.

Greenpeace Forest Views. http://www.greenpeace.org, Spring 2004.

Gripne, Stephanie and Hal Herring. "Model Grassbanking Projects." *The Nature Conservancy Magazine,* Spring 2004.

Gunawan, Marius. "Alliance Helps Overcome Indonesia's Forest Crisis." *The Jakarta Post*, April 27, 2004, www.thejakartapost.com.

Hamilton, Gordon. "Corporate Buyers Looks to Eco-Certified Forest Companies." *Vancouver Sun*, March 15, 2003.

———. "Preserve Half of Rainforest, Scientists Urge." *Vancouver Sun*, November 20, 2003, A3.

Hawkins, Paul. *The Ecology of Commerce*. New York: Harper Business, 1993.

Herring, Hal. "Fair Trade Ranchers Bank on Conservation." *Nature Conservancy Magazine*, Spring 2004.

Hopper, Kim and Ernest Cook. *Conservation Finance Handbook: How Communities Are Paying for Parks and Land Conservation*. San Francisco: The Trust For Public Land, 2004.

Hume, Mark. "You Don't Know What You Got Till it's Gone." *The Globe and Mail*, February 24, 2004.

Ingerson, Ann. *Conservation Capital: Sources of Private Funding for Forest Conservation*. The Wilderness Society, February 18, 2004.

Irland, Lloyd C. *The Northeast's Changing Forest*. Petersham MA: Harvard University Press, 1999.

Irland, Lloyd. "The Future of Large Forest Ownerships", presentation to Allegheny Section, Society of American Foresters given in Dover, Delaware on Feb. 19, 2004.

Jaeger, W. K. *Potential Benefits of Water Banks and Water Transfers*. Corvallis: Oregon State University, January 2004.

Karkos, Terry. "Federal Money to Help Preserve Wildlife Habitat." *Sun Journal* (Lewiston, Maine), March 4, 2004.

Kelda Group. News Updates. www.keldagroup.com/news/nrinterim_03.html/, accessed April 21, 2004.

Kestenbaum, Stuart. *Pilgrimage*. Portland, ME: Coyote Love Press, 1990.

Klinkenborg, Verlyn. "Crossing Borders." *Audubon* (Sept./Oct. 1995):34+.

Koberstein, Paul. *Cascadia Times*. Portland, OR: Cascadia Times Publishing Co., Summer 2003.

Lee, Peter, Dmitry Aksenov, Lars Laestadius, Ruth Nogueron, and Wynet Smith.

Canada's Large Intact Forest Landscapes. Edmonton, Alberta, Canada: Global Forest Watch, 2003.

Lindenmayer, David and Jerry Franklin. *Conserving Forest Biodiversity.* Washington, D.C.: Island Press, 2002.

"LIP program highlights struggle over which species need help" *Land Letter,* March 11, 2003.

Loucks, Andrea. *Strengthening the Ties that Bind.* Washington, D.C.: The Community Strategies Group, The Aspen Institute, 2002.

MacKinnon, J. B. "The Naked Truth about Great Bear Rainforest." *Explore,* September 2003, 38–43.

Malpai Borderlands Group End of Year Report. Accessed from www.malpaiborderlandsgroup.org, December, 2000.

McCallum, Rob and Nikhil Sekhran. *Race for the Rainforest: Evaluating Lessons from an Integrated Conservation and Development "Experiment" in New Ireland, Papua New Guinea.* Waigani, Papua New Guinea: PNG Biodiversity Conservation and Resource Management Programme, 1997.

McCrea, Peter. *Outlook on Forestry in Papua New Guinea.* Boroko, Papua New Guinea: National Forest Service.

McMahon, Janet. *An Ecological Reserves System Inventory: Potential Ecological Reserves on Maine's Existing Public and Private Conservation Lands.* Maine State Planning Office, July 1998.

McQueen, Mike, and Ed McMahon. *Land Conservation Financing.* Washington, D.C.: Island Press, 2003.

McQueen, Mike. *Common Ground.* Arlington, VA: The Conservation Fund, January–March 2004.

National Report on Sustainable Forests 2003 (Final Draft). Washington, D.C.: U.S. Department of Agriculture, Forest Service, November 8, 2002.

"The Nature Conservancy Discovers Large Population of Orangutans in Borneo." *The Nature Conservancy Magazine,* Winter 2002. Online at http://nature.org/magazine.

The Nature Conservancy. *Advocating for Climate Change Policy in U.S. States.* 2004.

———. "Chapter Helps Protect 15,370 Acres." Press release, April 21, 2004.

———. Heart Mt. Grassbank, Business Plan. December 2002, unpublished.

———. *Incentives for Greenhouse Gas Reductions throughout Carbon Sequestration: State-Level Activities.* March 11, 2004, unpublished research paper.

———. "Nature Conservancy over Halfway to Kelda Fundraising Goal." Middletown, CT, press release, March 28, 2002.

———. *Report on Field Work in Josephstaal.* November 1998.

———. *Supplementary Materials Sustainable Forestry Project Papua New Guinea.* Arlington, VA, November 2, 1997.

———. *Virginia Coast Reserve Program Assessment—August 2002, Final Report.* Arlington, VA, unpublished.

———. *Virginia Coast Reserve Program Assessment Executive Summary.* August, 2002.

Northern Forest Center. *Northern Forest Center Annual Report 2002.* Concord, NH, 2002.

O'Connell, Mike. *Tenaja Area Wildlife Linkage Preserve Design Plan.* Fax transmitted to author, May 21, 2004.

Ottaway, David B. and Joe Stephens. "On Eastern Shore, For-Profit Flagship Hits Shoals: Local Ventures Launched, Foundered and Failed." *Washington Post*, May 5, 2003, A11.

Patel-Weynand, Toral. *Biodiversity and Sustainable Forestry: State of the Science Review.* Washington, D.C.: The National Commission on Science for Sustainable Forestry, 2002.

Perschel, Robert T. *The Land Ethic Tool Box: Using Ethics, Emotion and Spiritual Values to Advance American Land Conservation.* The Wilderness Society, January 2004.

Postal, Sandra and Brian Richter. *Rivers for Life: Managing Water for People and Nature.* Washington, D.C.: Island Press, 2004.

Progress on the Back Forty. Washington, D.C.: Environmental Defense Fund, 2000.

"Publicly Owned Grassbanks: Just another Bailout." Accessed from www.publiclandsranching.org/htmlress/fs_grassbanks_no_good.htm, April 29, 2004.

Pye-Smith, Charlie and Carole Saint-Laurent. "Introduction to the Demonstration Portfolio." *Global Partnership on Forest Landscape Restoration: Investing in People and Nature.* See www.unep-wcmc.org/forest/restoration/globalpartnership/.

Rainforest Solutions. Vancouver, B.C.: Rainforest Solutions Project, Winter 2004. See www.savethegreatbear.org.

Rawlins, Wade. "N.C. Forests Falling Fast: State Lost More than 1 Million Acres from 1990 to 2002." *North Carolina News and Observer*, March 26, 2004.

Redford, Kent H., and Jane A. Mansour, eds. *Traditional Peoples and Biodiversity Conservation in Large Tropical Landscapes*. Arlington, VA: The Nature Conservancy, 1996.

Refkin, David. *Toward a Greener Forest Products Industry*. Presentation notes, November 17, 2003.

Rolde, Neil. *The Baxters of Maine: Downeast Visionaries*. Gardiner, ME: Tilbury House Publishers, 1997.

Rolde, Neil. *The Interrupted Forest: A History of Maine's Wildlands*. Gardiner, ME: Tilbury House Publishers, 2001.

Salafsky, Nick, Bernd Cordes, John Parks, and Cheryl Hochman. *Evaluating Linkages between Business and the Environment and Local Communities*. Washington, D.C.: Biodiversity Support Program, 1999.

Saulei, Simon. "Natural Regeneration Following Clear-Fell Logging Operations in the Gogol Valley, Papua New Guinea." *Ambio* 13, 5–6 (1984).

Sauls, Edwin G. "Practical Tips for Developers" *Developers Guide to Endangered Species Regulation*. Washington, D.C.: National Homebuilders Association, 1996.

Seddon, George. "Logging in the Gogol Valley, Papua New Guinea." *Ambio* 13, 5–6 (1984).

Sizer, Nigel. *How the @#%* Can TNC Combat Illegal Logging in Indonesia?!*. Powerpoint presentation. The Nature Conservancy.

Social Investment Forum. *2003 Report on Socially Responsible Investing Trends in the United States*. Washington, D.C., December.

State of the Worlds Forests 2003. Rome: Food and Agriculture Organization of the United Nations, 2003.

Steinzon, Nadia. "Exploring Educational Approaches to Advance Landscape-Scale Conservation." Bard Center for Environmental Policy, master's thesis, May 2004.

Stuart, Marc and Nikhil Sekhran. *Developing Externally Financed Greenhouse Gas Mitigation Projects in Papua New Guinea's Forestry Sector: A Review of*

Concepts, Opportunities and Links to Biodiversity Conservation. Port Moresby, Papua New Guinea: PNG Biodiversity Conservation and Resource Management Programme, September 1996.

Tabis, Phil. "Making the Case for State Tax Incentives for Private Land Conservation." *Land Trust Alliance Exchange,* Spring 1999.

———. *State Conservation Tax Incentives—Summary of Approaches and Current Status.* Arlington, VA: The Nature Conservancy, unpublished

Timberland Markets. North Hollywood, CA: Paperloop December 2003.

Timberland Markets. North Hollywood, CA: Paperloop August 2004.

Two Countries, One Forest: Protecting and Connecting Nature from New York to Nova Scotia. Conference Notes 2C1F Montreal Meeting held May 17–18, 2004.

United Nations Development Programme. *World Resources 2000–2001: People and Ecosystems—The Fraying Web of Life.* Oxford, England: Elsevier Science, 2000.

Urquhart, Thomas. *For the Beauty of the Earth: Birding Opera and other Journeys.* Washington, D.C.: Shoemaker and Hoard, 2004.

Wayburn, Laurie, Jerry F. Franklin, John C. Gordon, Clark S. Binkly, David J. Mladenoff, and Norman L. Christensen. *Forest Carbon in the United States: Opportunities and Options for Private Lands.* Santa Rosa, CA: Pacific Forest Trust, Fall 2000.

Weeks, William. *Beyond the Ark.* Washington, D.C.: Island Press, 1997.

Wild East: The Newsletter of CPAWS Nova Scotia. Canadian Parks and Wilderness Society, Spring 2004.

Wilson, E. O. *The Future of Life.* New York: Knopf, 2002.

World Wide Fund for Nature. *Guidelines for Investment in Operations that Impact Forests.* September 2003.

Yellowstone to Yukon Conservation Initiative. *Yellowstone to Yukon: A Blueprint for Wildlife Conservation.*

Zinn, Jeffrey. "Funding Trends for Selected Resource Conservation Programs." *Renewable Resources Journal* (Spring 2004):4–10.

Index

Additionality concept and carbon issues, 85, 86–87
Adirondack Forest Preserve, 170
Advocacy work and socially responsible investing, 67
Agriculture and incentives for working landscapes, 142–45, 148–49
Agriculture Department, U.S., 142, 144
American Can/Primerica, 68
American Electric Power (AEP), 78
Anderson, Mark, 172
Anderson, Terry, 69
Another Turn of the Crank (Berry), 157
Appalachian Trail, 166, 177
Arizona and tax credits for conservation, 128, 131
Army Corps of Engineers, U.S., 140
Arnovon Islands and conservation failure, 161–62

Bank of nature:
    forestbanks, 100–102
    grassbanking, 93–98
    resources for the, 103
    summary/conclusions, 102–3
    water markets used for conservation, 96, 98–100
Bankruptcy and biodiversity, 53–61
Baxter, Percival P., 44, 170, 184
Baxter State Park, 44–46, 127
Bears, 113, 141
Bedard, Lambert, 42, 43
Belize, carbon mitigation in, 80
Berry, Wendell, 63
Beyond the Ark (Weeks), 138, 157
Big Walnut Nature Preserve, 84

Biodiversity Conservation Network (NCN), 161–63
Bolivia and forests/carbon emissions, 75–79
Bolivia Sustainable Forest Management Project (BOLFOR), 79
Boreal Forest Conservation Framework, 110
Bosques S.A., 53–54
Bottle/can recycling in Maine, 6–7
Bowater, 43
Brascan Financial, 49–50
Braun, E. Lucy, 84
Brazil, carbon mitigation in, 80
British Petroleum (BP), 78
Burlington Northern Company, 23
Business Ethics, 71
Business in the environment, importance of engaging, 5–13, 181–84
    see also individual subject headings

Calcareous soils of Northern Forest, 172
California:
    carbon issues, 82, 85, 89
    grassbanking, 98
    water markets used for conservation, 96, 98–99
CALPER, 25
Campbell Group, 25, 36
Canada's forests and greening business, 110–14
    see also Northern Forest
Capital Consultants, 59
Carbon and forests:
    additionality concept/test, 85, 86–87
    Chicago Climate Exchange, 81

Carbon and forests (continued)
    credits, carbon, 9
    leakage issues, 87
    Midwest Forest Restoration project,
        83–84
    Noel Kempff project in Bolivia, 75–79
    Pacific Forest Trust, 84–86
    partner test, 87
    permanence issues, 87
    problems with linking carbon mitiga-
        tion to conservation, 80–81
    resources for carbon projects, 88
    state (U.S.) initiatives on, 81–83, 89–91
Cattle and grassbanking, 93–96
CEI, see Coastal Enterprises Inc.
Center for Conservation Incentives,
    143–44
Center for Enterprise Development
    (CFED), 159
Certification process and greening busi-
    ness, 114–16, 177
Champion International, 27, 175
Chicago Climate Exchange (CCX), 81
Chile and bankruptcy/biodiversity,
    53–61
Cinergy Corporation, 84
Clean Development Mechanism (Kyoto
    Treaty), 80–81
Climate change, 4
    see also Carbon and forests
Climate Change Action Plan (2001), 82
Clinch Valley (VA) and forestbanks,
    101–3
Coalition for Environmentally Respon-
    sible Economics (CERES), 71
Coastal Enterprises Inc. (CEI), 63–67,
    72, 126–28, 131
Colorado:
    Landowner Incentive Program, 139
    tax credits for conservation, 123
Coming to Land in a Troubled World
    (Forbes), 1
Commodity Credit Corporation, 142–43
Community investing and socially re-
    sponsible investing, 67

Compatible development, see Failures,
    conservation
Compatible Ventures, 103
Conference of Parties (2004), 80
Connecticut:
    carbon issues, 89
    Northern Forest conservation,
        175–77
    water-supply protection, forestlands
        and, 119–22
Connecticut River, 175
Conservation Forest Capital, 36
Conservation Forest Partners, 72
Conservation Forestry, 69–70
Conservation Fund, The (TCF), 27, 31
Conservation International (CI), 57, 164
Conservation Reserve Enhancement
    Program (CREP), 145–46
Conservation Reserve Program (CRP),
    144–45
Conservation Security Program (CSP),
    146–47
Conserving Forest Biodiversity (Franklin
    & Lindenmayer), 59
Conti National Wildlife Refuge, 176
Convention on Biodiversity, 182
Credits for reducing carbon
    emissions, 77
"Crossing Borders: Good News from the
    Badlands" (Klinkenborg), 92
Cruchfield, Ed, 55, 56
Cyclosporine, 120

Daisy, 109
D'Alessandro, David F., 47
Dam relicensing, 100, 177
Debt for nature, 42–50
deBuys, William, 94
Development and declining
    forestlands, 5
Dickey Lincoln Dam, 1
Discounted loans, 51–52
Dogwood Alliance, 67
Domtar Inc., 110, 170
Doody, Eldon, 48

Draper, E. Lynn, 78
Drinking-water standards, 120

Easements and tax credits for conserva-
    tion, 124, 130
Ecological land units, 172
Economy (global), need to confront di-
    rection of the, 5
E Magazine, 66
Environmental Defense Fund (EDF):
    Center for Conservation Incentives,
        143–44
    contact information for, 103
    greening business, 116
    Mono Lake debate, 96, 98
    perverse incentives, impact of, 137
    safe harbor/no surprise agreements
        with landowners, 139
Environmental Quality Incentives Pro-
    gram (EQIP), 139–42, 147–48

Failures, conservation:
    Biodiversity Conservation Network,
        161–63
    lessons learned about compatible de-
        velopment, 166–67
    Papua New Guinea, 163–65
    Virginia Eastern Shore Sustainable
        Development Corporation,
        157–61
Farmland Protection Program (FPP),
    148–49
Farm Service Agency (FSA), 144
Federal Energy Regulatory Commission
    (FERC), 100
Fernandez, Carlos, 57
Ferret, black-footed, 95
Findling, Robert M., 124
Fish and Wildlife Service, U.S. (FWS),
    100, 140, 141
Fishbein, Greg, 55, 56, 58
Fish tag loans, 64–66
FleetBoston, 55, 56–57
Florida Power and Light (FPL), 177
Forbes, Peter, 183

Ford Foundation, 158
Forestbanks, 100–102
Forest Capital Partners, 36–37
Forest Investment Associates, 37
Forestland Group, 38
Forest Service, U.S., 4
Forest Stewardship Council (FSC), 114,
    115, 118
Forest Systems, 37
Fox, swift, 95
Fundación Amigos de la Naturaleza
    (FAN), 78

GE Capital, 127–28
Georgia Pacific, 21, 43
Gifford, Chad, 55
Gilges, Kent, 70
Glickman, Marsha, 66
Global Climate Change Initiative, 88
Global Conservation Fund (GCF), 57
Global Program of Action on Protected
    Areas, 80
GMO-Renewable Resources (GMO-
    RR), 31, 38, 176
Goldman Sachs, 59–61
Government spending on
    conservation, 5
Grantham and Mayo (GMO), 30
Grassbanking, 93–98
Grasslands declining in productivity,
    92–93
Grasslands Reserve Program (GRP),
    149–50
Gray Ranch (NM) and grassbanking, 97
Grazing and grassbanking, 93–98
Great Bear Rainforest, 111–13
Great Northern Paper Company, 42–
    50, 127
Great Remembering, The (Forbes), 119
Great Smoky National Park, 100
Great Work, The (Berry), 181
Greening business:
    Canada's forests, 110–14
    certification process, 114–16
    environmentally friendly products, 117

Greening business (continued)
    Indonesia, orangutans in, 107–10
    Northern Forest, 176–77
    resources, forest certification, 118
    TI Paperco Inc., 116–17
GreenMoney Journal, 71
Green Mountain Energy Company, 85
Green Mountain National Forest, 170
Gregg, Judd, 17
Gripne, Stephanie, 103
Grizzly bears, 141
Guthrie, Jim, 139

Habitat management and tax credits for
    conservation, 124
Habitat requirements for species, fickle,
    136–37
Hadley, Drum, 93
Hancock Life Insurance Company, 22,
    45–48
Hancock Timber Resources, 22, 25, 29,
    38–39
Hawkins, Paul, 107, 181
Haynes, H. C., 32–33
Heart Mountain Ranch (WY) and grass-
    banking, 95–97
Hines, Ken, 47
Holland-Indonesia connection and
    greening business, 108–9
Home Depot, 109, 113
Houghton, David, 19

IBM Business Consulting Services, 117
Idaho and carbon issues, 90
IKEA, 113
Incentives for working landscapes:
    agricultural programs, 142–45,
        148–49
    Center for Conservation Incentives,
        143–44
    Environmental Quality Incentives
        Program, 139–42
    federal government programs
        Conservation Reserve Enhance-
            ment Program, 145–46

Conservation Reserve Program,
    144–45
Conservation Security Program,
    146–47
Environment Quality Incentives
    Program, 147–48
Farmland Protection Program,
    148–49
Grasslands Reserve Program,
    149–50
Landowner Incentives Program,
    152–53
Wetlands Reserve Program, 150–51
Wildlife Habitat Incentives Pro-
    gram, 151–52
habitat requirements for species,
    fickle, 136–37
Landowner Incentive Program, 138–39
overview, 7
perverse incentives, impact of, 137–38
safe harbor/no surprise agreements
    with landowners, 139
transformative way to a new econ-
    omy, 143–44
see also Greening business; Tax credits
    for conservation
Indiana and carbon issues, 84
Indonesia:
    failure, conservation, 162
    greening business and orangutans,
        107–10
International Paper (IP):
    forestlands set up as separate business
        ventures, 21
    greening business and certification
        process, 115
    Machias River area in Maine, 32–33
    New Hampshire forestland sale,
        17–20, 27
    Northern Forest, 169–70, 175–77
    St. John River Project in Maine, 2
Investment banking for conservation:
    bankruptcy and biodiversity, 53–61
    debt for nature, 42–50
    overview of, 62

see also Socially responsible investing;
    Timber, partnering with big
IP, *see* International Paper

Juniper Hills Preserve, 98
Justiniano, Hermes, 75

Katahdin Forest and debt for nature,
    42–50
Kelda, 119–22, 124, 126
Kelly, Marjorie, 66
Kennedy, Robert F., Jr., 53
Kermode bear, 113
Kyoto Treaty, 78, 80–81

Landowner Incentive Program (LIP),
    138–39, 152–53
Land Trust Alliance, 126–127, 130
Large-scale conservation, 4–5, 25–26
    see also Northern Forest
Leakage issues and carbon sequestra-
    tion, 87
Legislation:
    Endangered Species Act (ESA) of
        1973, 1, 139
    Farm Bill of 1996, 139
Leighton, Martin, 117
Levesque, Charlie, 19
Limited partnerships as new way of
    owning timberlands, 22
Livermore, David, 99
Loans, buying, 45–52
Lore Lindu National Park, 162
Los Angles (CA) and water markets used
    for conservation, 98–99
Lousewort, furbish, 1–4
Low, Greg, 100–101
Lowes, 109
Lyme Timber Company, 19–20, 39,
    67–69, 72
Lyons Falls Pulp & Paper, 30

Machias River, 32–33
Maine:
    bottle/can recycling, 6–7

carbon issues, 83, 90
    fish industry's sustainability, 63
    fish tag loans, 64–66
    forestland lost in, 5
    greening business and certification
        process, 114–15
    Katahdin Forest and debt for nature,
        42–50
    Landowner Incentive Program,
        138–39
    Machias River area, 32–33
    Northern Forest conservation, 175–77
    St. John River Project, 1–4, 27–28
Malpai Borderlands Group, 94
Market-based tools for conservation,
    5–13, 181–84
    see also individual subject headings
Maryland and tax credits for conserva-
    tion, 124–25
Massachusetts and carbon issues, 90
Matador Ranch and grassbanking, 98
McKeague, Marcia, 45
Mead-Westvaco, 115, 177
Midwest Forest Restoration project,
    83–84
Milwaukee, contaminated drinking
    water in, 120
Minnesota and carbon issues, 90
Missouri River, 140–41
Moellenbrock, Bonny, 124
Molpus Woodlands Group, 39
Mono Lake, 96, 98–99
Montana:
    grassbanking, 97, 98
    grizzly bears/trout habitat, improv-
        ing, 141
    sturgeon, saving the pallid, 140–41
Morgan, Tim, 42–43
Morgan Stanley, 59
Mouse, Preble's Meadow jumping, 139

Nash State Forest, 177
National Audubon Society, 96
National Implementation Support Part-
    nership (NISP), 79–80

Natural Resources Conservation Service (NRCS), 140–42
Nature Conservancy, The (TNC):
  carbon issues, 84, 88
  Chile and bankruptcy/biodiversity, 53–61
  Coastal Enterprises, partnership with, 127–28
  critical look at, 13
  failure, conservation, 163–65
  forestbanks, 101–2
  grassbanking, 93
  greening business, 108–9
  insider sales, allegations of, 126
  IP selling forestland in New Hampshire, 19, 20
  Katahdin Forest and debt for nature, 42–50
  Lyme Timber Company, 67–68
  Machias River area in Maine, 32–33
  St. John River Project in Maine, 1–4, 27
  tax credits for conservation, 121–22, 126–28
  Tug Hill project in NY, 28–31
  Virginia Eastern Shore Sustainable Development Corporation, 157–61
  waterbanking, 99–100
Nearing, Helen, 7
Nearing, Scott, 7
Nebraska and carbon issues, 90
Net present value (NPV), 51–52
Nevada and water markets used for conservation, 99–100
New Economy of Nature, The (Daily & Ellison), 17, 136
New Hampshire:
  carbon issues, 91
  IP selling land in, 17–20, 27
  Northern Forest conservation, 175–77
New Jersey and carbon issues, 82
New Market Tax Credit (NMTC), 126–31
New Mexico:
  grassbanking, 97

grassland productivity declines, 92
  tax credits for conservation, 123–24
New York:
  carbon issues, 83
  Tug Hill project, 28–31
  water-supply protection, purchasing forestlands for, 120–21
Noel Kempff Mercado National Park, 75–79
North Carolina:
  forestland lost in, 5
  tax credits for conservation, 122–23
Northeastern Wilds (Gorman), 168
Northeast Regional Greenhouse Gas Initiative, 81, 89
Northern Forest:
  breeding pairs of key species, land for, 173
  connecting areas of forest blocks for wide-ranging species, 173, 175
  disturbance from natural causes, 172
  greening business, 176–77
  major conservation projects (1990/2002), 179
  new strategy/vision for the future, 171–73
  old-growth systems, 172–73
  overview, 168
  private companies, long history of use by, 168–69, 176
  resources for, 180
  revisions mandated by economic forces, 170–71
  scaling factors for reserves in, 174
  summary/conclusions, 177–78
  tristate area of Vermont/New Hampshire/Maine, 175–77
  turnover in land ownership, 169–70
  water resources, valuing, 176
Northern Forest Alliance, 180
Northern Forest Center, 180

Office Depot, 67
Old-growth systems in Northern Forest, 172–73

Orangutans, 107–10
Oregon:
    carbon issues, 91
    grassbanking, 98

Pacific Forest Trust (PFT), 84–86, 88
PacifiCorp, 78
Paper industry and greening business,
    116–17
Papua New Guinea and conservation
    failure, 163–65
Paraguay, conservation failure in, 164
Partner test and carbon issues, 87
Pataki, George E., 82
Paulson, Hank, 47, 60
Pepin, Ray, 8
Permanence issues and carbon seques-
    tration, 87
Perverse incentives, impact of, 137–38
Phillips, Ron, 70
Pingree family and Northern Forest,
    175, 177
Plum Creek Timber Company, 23, 25, 40
Pollan, Michael, 182
Poole, Lynda, 95
Portland Press Herald, 184
Postel, Sandra, 77
Prairie dogs, 95
Property and Environmental Research
    Center (PERC), 69
Property rights, absolute, 94
Prudential Timber, 40

Quinn, Dan, 75, 76
Quinn, Jim, 115

Rainforest Action Network (RAN),
    55, 67
Rangeley Lakes Land Trust, 177
Real estate investment trusts (REITs),
    21–26
Recreational access, 31
Refkin, David, 116, 117
Renewable Resources, 30
Resource Conservation Services, 9

Rethinking Environmentalism (Du-
    manoski), 42
Richter, Brian, 77
Rio Condor project in Chile, 58–61
RMK Timberland Group, 40–41
Rogers, Will, 19
Royer, Raymond, 111
Rumpf, Tom, 32–33, 45

St. John River project, 1–4, 27–28
Sanders, Scott R., 114, 178
Sandor, Richard, 75
Scale of nature, need to work at, 4–5,
    26–27
    see also Northern Forest
Screening and socially responsible in-
    vesting, 66
S.D. Warren Company, 8–9
Seven Islands Land Company, 176
Shaheen, Jean, 17
Shareholder advocacy and socially re-
    sponsible investing, 66–67
Sheehan, Elizabeth, 63–65
Shoshone National Forest, 96
Sizer, Nigel, 108, 110
Social Investment Forum, 71
Socially responsible investing (SRI):
    Coastal Enterprises' mission, 63–67
    core strategies, 66–67
    fish tag loans, 64–66
    funds/managers, investment, 72
    growth of, 66
    Lyme Timber Company, 67–69
    nonprofit organizations not trusted
        by investors, 68
    periodicals dealing with, 71
    power of equity, 70–71
    questionable environmental records
        of companies targeted, 67
    Tomlin, John, 69–70
    watchdog/research organizations, 71
    see also Greening business
Society for the Protection of New
    Hampshire Forests, 19
Solis, Francisco, 57

Solomon Islands and conservation fail-
    ure, 161–62
Stanley, Bill, 81–82
Stein, Peter, 67–68
Stewart, Gary, 110
Stillwater National Wildlife Refuge, 99
Strugar, Mike, 124
Stuart Land and Cattle Company, 101, 102
Sturgeon, pallid, 140–41
Sumalindo Lestari Jaya, 109
Suncor Energy, 110
Sun River Basin (MT) and grassbank-
    ing, 97
Sustainable Forest Initiative (SFI), 115,
    118, 177
Sutherland, David, 119–20, 122
Syre, David, 58, 61

Tabas, Phil, 60, 125
Targeted investing, see Socially responsi-
    ble investing
Tax credits for conservation:
    Arizona, 128, 131
    Coastal Enterprises-TNC partnership,
        127–28
    Colorado, 123
    easements and donations of land,
        124–25, 130
    federal incentives, 125–28
    GE Capital and TNC-CEI, partner-
        ship of, 128
    New Market Tax Credit, 126–31
    New Mexico, 124–25
    North Carolina, 122–23
    overview, 130
    summary of state/federal, 132–35
    three approaches to state incentives,
        125
    water-supply protection, forestlands
        and, 119–22
Tecklin, David, 57
Tembec, 110
Tennessee, splitting ownership of
    trees/land in, 31

Timber, partnering with big:
    balancing goals of conservation with
        expectations of private in-
        vestors, 33
    comparing St. John River project and
        IP's New Hampshire purchases,
        27
    growing number of partnerships,
        20–21
    IP selling forestland in New Hamp-
        shire, 17–20
    key concepts in partnering with pri-
        vate capital, 34–35
    large properties, need for conserva-
        tionists to buy, 26–27
    Machias River area in Maine, 32–33
    organizations, guide to timber invest-
        ment, 36–41
    real estate investment trusts, 21–26
    short time land ownership patterns, 25
    Tennessee land sale and splitting
        ownership of trees/land, 31–32
    timber investment and management
        organizations, 21–26
    Tug Hill project in NY, 28–31
    see also Greening business
Timber investment and management
    organizations (TIMOs), 21–26
Time Warner and greening business,
    116–17
TI Paperco Inc., 116–17
TNC, see Nature Conservancy, The
Tomlin, John, 69–70
Treasury Department, U.S., 127
Trillium Corporation, 58–61
Trout, 141
Trust for Public Land (TPL), 18–20, 67–69
Tug Hill project in NY, 28–31
Two Countries, One Forest, 180

Umbagog National Wildlife Refuge, 177
United States:
    Bolivian forest management, giving
        aid to, 79

carbon issues, state initiatives on, 81–83, 89–91
Kyoto treaty, opposition to, 78, 80
see also individual states

Valle Grande (NM) grassbanking project, 97
Vermont:
carbon issues, 85
Northern Forest conservation, 175–77
Vina Plains Preserve, 98
Vireo, black-capped, 137
Virginia and forestbanks, 101–3
Virginia Eastern Shore Sustainable Development Corporation (VESC), 157–61

Wagner Forest Management, 41
Ward, Jared, 55–57
Warming, global, 4
Washington Post, 125–26
Waste products, recycling, 8–9
Water markets used for conservation, 96, 98–100
Water resources in Northern Forest, 176

Water-supply protection, forestlands and, 119–22
Weeks, Bill, 100–101, 138, 157, 160–61
Wetlands Reserve Program (WRP), 150–51
Weyerhaeuser, 163–64
White Mountain National Forest, 170, 172
Wieman, Allan, 127
Wildlife Conservation Society, 61
Wildlife Habitat Incentives Program (WHIP), 151–52
William, John, 64–65
Wilson, E. O., 13
Winrock International, 88
Wolkoff, Dennis, 60
Wommack, Kent, 2, 42–43
Woodlands Development Corporation, 53
Woodlots and forestbanks, 100–102
Woody species increasing at expense of grass, 92–93
World Bank, 164
World Wildlife Fund, 55, 57, 108
Wyoming and grassbanking, 95–97

Yellowstone National Park, 182

Island Press Board of Directors

Victor M. Sher, Esq. *(Chair)*
Sher & Leff
San Francisco, CA

Dane A. Nichols *(Vice-Chair)*
Washington, DC

Carolyn Peachey *(Secretary)*
Campbell, Peachey & Associates
Washington, DC

Drummond Pike *(Treasurer)*
President
The Tides Foundation
San Francisco, CA

Robert E. Baensch
Director, Center for Publishing
New York University
New York, NY

David C. Cole
President
Aquaterra, Inc.
Washington, VA

Catherine M. Conover
Quercus LLC
Washington, DC

Merloyd Ludington
Merloyd Lawrence, Inc.
Boston, MA

William H. Meadows
President
The Wilderness Society
Washington, DC

Henry Reath
Princeton, NJ

Will Rogers
President
The Trust for Public Land
San Francisco, CA

Alexis G. Sant
Trustee and Treasurer
Summit Foundation
Washington, DC

Charles C. Savitt
President
Island Press
Washington, DC

Susan E. Sechler
Senior Advisor
The German Marshall Fund
Washington, DC

Peter R. Stein
General Partner
LTC Conservation Advisory Services
The Lyme Timber Company
Hanover, NH

Diana Wall, Ph.D.
Director and Professor
Natural Resource Ecology Laboratory
Colorado State University
Fort Collins, CO

Wren Wirth
Washington, DC